Jeremy Wagner

RESPONS
JAVASCRIPT

MORE FROM A BOOK APART

Design for Safety
Eva PenzeyMoog

Voice Content and Usability
Preston So

Better Onboarding
Krystal Higgins

Sustainable Web Design
Tom Greenwood

Design for Cognitive Bias
David Dylan Thomas

Cross-Cultural Design
Senongo Akpem

Expressive Design Systems
Yesenia Perez-Cruz

Resilient Management
Lara Hogan

Everyday Information Architecture
Lisa Maria Marquis

Progressive Web Apps
Jason Grigsby

Visit abookapart.com for our full list of titles.

Copyright © 2021 Jeremy Wagner
All rights reserved

Publisher: Jeffrey Zeldman
Designer: Jason Santa Maria
Executive director: Katel LeDû
Managing editor: Lisa Maria Marquis
Editors: Sally Kerrigan, Adaobi Obi Tulton, Caren Litherland
Technical editor: Mat Marquis
Book producer: Ron Bilodeau

ISBN: 978-1-952616-15-0

A Book Apart
New York, New York
http://abookapart.com

10 9 8 7 6 5 4 3 2 1

TABLE OF CONTENTS

1 — CHAPTER 1
JavaScript: Handle with Care

15 — CHAPTER 2
Fast from the Start

46 — CHAPTER 3
Measuring and Assessing JavaScript Performance

73 — CHAPTER 4
Building for Speed

109 — CHAPTER 5
Navigating Toolchains

134 — CHAPTER 6
Smoother Runtime Performance

158 — CHAPTER 7
Managing Third-Party JavaScript

180 — *Conclusion*

181 — *Acknowledgments*

183 — *Resources*

186 — *References*

194 — *Index*

To Zandy, Maya, Lucy, Groant, and Mowzers.

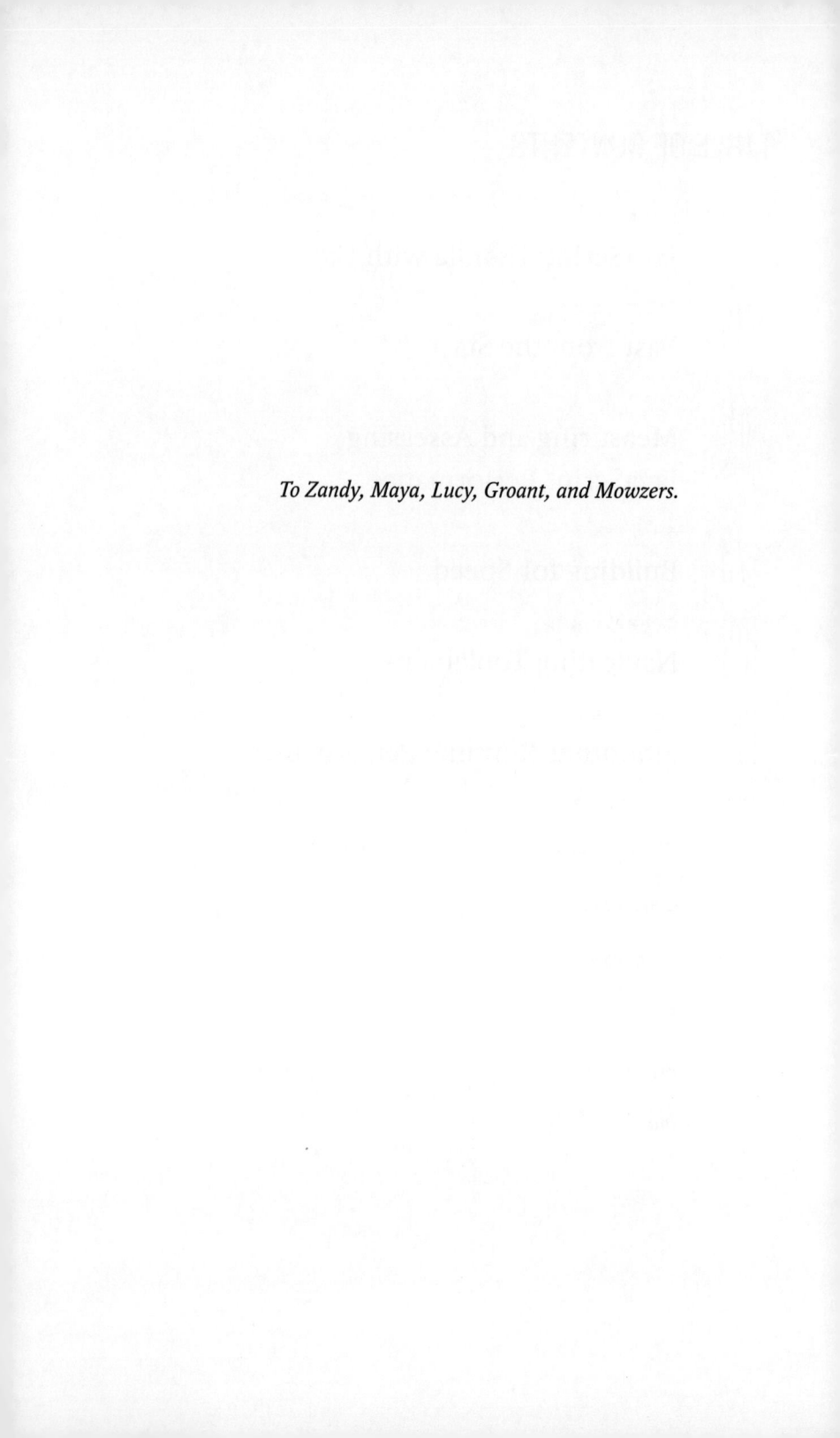

FOREWORD

WE ALL WANT USERS TO HAVE the fast, smooth web experience they expect, whether they're using a phone, tablet, or laptop. But competing interests often intervene. Developers want an interesting development experience. Designers want a beautiful and crisp design. Program managers want detailed user interaction reports to test what works. Advertisers want to track, well, everything.

It can feel impossible to balance all these needs while also cutting costs and speeding up the development process—and, sadly, the frameworks and libraries we turn to for help can have a negative impact on accessibility, security, web performance, and the user experience.

If we truly want to deliver a great experience to our users, we must be better stewards of usability and performance—which is exactly what Jeremy can teach us. With over fifteen years of experience developing websites and applications for projects large and small, Jeremy has a sharp understanding of how to strike a balance between business requirements, user needs, and developer interests. He takes a big-picture approach, explaining not just the how of using JavaScript thoughtfully, but also the why. By learning from diverse, real-world examples, you'll be able to envision what makes sense for your own projects, and build a high-performing, optimal experience for your users.

You'll also learn more than you ever wanted to know about wasps. Hopefully that information is never needed.

—**Estelle Weyl**

1
JAVASCRIPT: HANDLE WITH CARE

WARNING: THIS BOOK CONTAINS excessive metaphors about wasps, which may be unsettling.

Let's kick this off with *Sphex*, the first of many wasps we'll meet.

Sphex is a genus of solitary wasps that nest underground and prey on crickets (**FIG 1.1**). When one of these wasps brings a cricket back to its nest, it does something uncharacteristically thoughtful: the wasp conducts a nest inspection, leaving the cricket outside. Once the wasp finishes, it reemerges to retrieve the cricket.

Now for the kicker: if you—a prankster god of insectkind—move the cricket during the nest inspection, the wasp's behavioral program reboots. The wasp knows only that the cricket wasn't where it once was, so the wasp relocates it, drags it back to the nest entrance, and inspects the nest *again*.

While this behavior isn't consistent across digger wasps, the concept offers rhetorical usefulness by way of a word coined by scholar Douglas Hofstadter: *sphexishness* (http://bkaprt.com/rjs39/01-03). When we say something is sphexish, we're describing highly deterministic, preprogrammed behavior that has the *appearance* of thoughtfulness. I often grumble to myself about

FIG 1.1: A wasp identified as *Sphex pensylvanicus*. Photograph by Hardyplants (http://bkaprt.com/rjs39/01-01), CC0 1.0 (http://bkaprt.com/rjs39/01-02), via Wikimedia Commons.

our industry's sphexishness and the effect it has had on the collective usability of the web.

You didn't fork out fun money for this book to be told that you're a drone incapable of critical thought—and that's certainly not the case. We all strive to do our work the best way we know how. Yet we do many small, almost ceremoniously repetitive things as web developers that are definitely sphexish.

Consider our relentless adherence to best practices, even when they result in poor user experiences. We `npm install` packages without considering potential downsides or alternative methods. We chase new tools in the hope that they'll increase our productivity—even though that constant churn invites its own insidious productivity cost.

2 RESPONSIBLE JAVASCRIPT

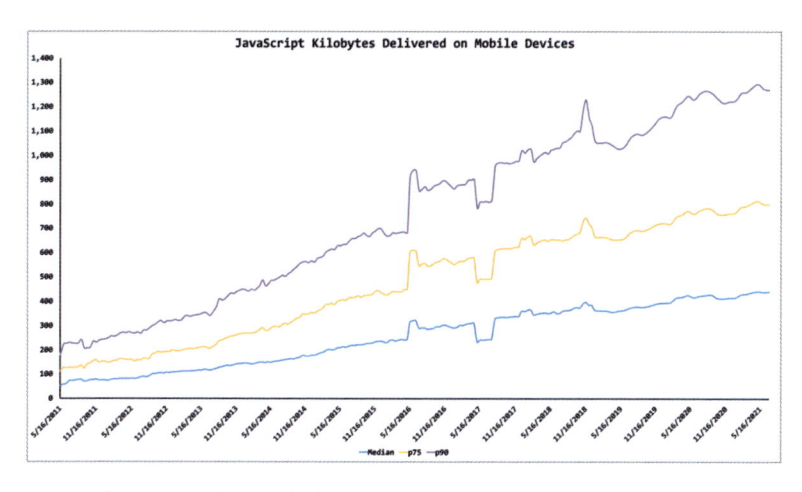

FIG 1.2: This HTTP Archive graph shows the median, 75th, and 90th percentiles of JavaScript payloads delivered to mobile devices. From 2012 to 2021, 10 percent of websites have gone from shipping 200 kilobytes of JavaScript to shipping nearly 1.25 megabytes (http://bkaprt.com/rjs39/01-04).

We just do a lot of *stuff* that results in bad outcomes for the people who use what we make. It's a bold assertion, yes, but one that's well supported by data: there's been a fivefold increase in the amount of JavaScript that websites have sent from 2012 to 2020 (**FIG 1.2**).

We sometimes celebrate when lines on graphs go up; this isn't one of those times. Increasing the amount of JavaScript we ship results in poor user experiences and violates the Priority of Constituencies (http://bkaprt.com/rjs39/01-05):

> *In case of conflict, consider users over authors over implementors over specifiers over theoretical purity.*

This quote hits bluntly: users always come first. Our preferences and comfort as developers are secondary. That's a mission to take to heart while we figure out how we can use JavaScript more responsibly in an industry that relies on it more than ever.

JAVASCRIPT'S ROLE IN PERFORMANCE

Using JavaScript responsibly first requires an understanding of how browsers process it. It's tempting to reduce a website's performance to its transfer size.

Yes, the page that sends fewer bytes will typically be faster than the one that sends more—given identical conditions, anyway. Yet this isn't the only factor for web performance. In reality, there are two: loading performance and runtime performance.

Loading performance

Loading performance is how quickly an HTML document and its assets—CSS, images, and, yes, JavaScript—arrive over the network after the browser requests them. All we can control when it comes to loading performance is what we send, how much of it we send, and how we send it. Much of what affects loading performance occurs beyond our control, in that chasm between the browser and the web server.

Despite this, we have a few tricks at our disposal to improve loading performance:

- *Minification*, which culls unnecessary spaces and comments from text assets such as HTML, CSS, and JavaScript files to reduce their size. Minification is effective since it takes advantage of the fact that computers don't require such luxuries to run the code we write.
- *Compression*, which is when the server reduces text asset size via a compression algorithm prior to sending it to the browser. Think ZIP files, except assets are compressed before being sent and are decompressed after they arrive over the network.

We seem to consistently get minification and compression right because they're easily automated either by build processes or by servers. It's that stuff we *can't* automate that makes using JavaScript responsibly a tall order—the biggest task of which involves managing what happens *after* the browser requests and receives JavaScript assets.

> 459 requests | 5.2 MB transferred | 13.6 MB resources

FIG 1.3: Google Chrome's developer tools summarize assets in the Network tab. From left to right are the total number of requested assets, their transfer size (including compression), and their actual (decompressed) size.

Runtime performance

Runtime performance describes how responsive a page is to input once it appears in the browser. When a page is persistently slow to respond to interactions, we say that page's runtime performance is poor.

Remember all that talk about compression a bit ago? Whatever is compressed must be decompressed. Browser developer tools reflect this by reporting both the *transfer size* (presumably compressed) and the *actual size* (decompressed) of assets (FIG 1.3).

If this seems inconsequential, consider that if a 200-kilobyte compressed JavaScript asset decompresses to 800 kilobytes, the browser must process those 800 kilobytes of script! Processing JavaScript, as you'll see, is a whole other hornets' nest.

The cost of processing JavaScript

The drudgework of how browsers handle JavaScript isn't so much in the downloading but in the processing of it. Browser vendors constantly hack away on JavaScript engines to improve their performance in ways we web developers can't. Despite such improvements, processing JavaScript is a spendy endeavor that gets more expensive the slower the device.

Reducing web performance to a question of bytes assumes that every byte has the same performance cost. This is true of loading performance, but not runtime performance, where processing a byte of JavaScript requires more computational effort than a byte of, say, CSS.

Let's illustrate this point with data: after querying and analyzing seventy-two million Lighthouse audits performed in 2020 in HTTP Archive's BigQuery store (http://bkaprt.com/rjs39/01-

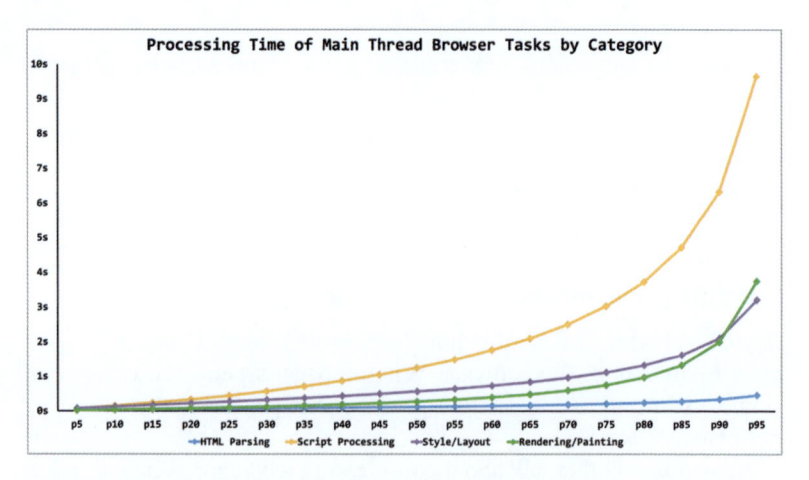

FIG 1.4: CPU processing time for JavaScript worsens at higher percentiles where Lighthouse audits encountered pages with larger JavaScript payloads. In the median case, processors spent over ten times as long processing JavaScript as they did HTML.

06), it became evident that, across these audits, CPU time spent processing JavaScript far exceeded CPU time spent on style/layout operations, HTML, and rendering/painting (**FIG 1.4**).

Considering this data, we can see how a good chunk of the web is acceptably fast for those relative few on high-end hardware, sluggishly irritating for the middling many, and downright unusable for those on low-end hardware.

If it's tempting to handwave away the problem of slow devices, check out the best-selling unlocked mobile phone on Amazon at the time of this writing: a $60 BLU Studio Mini phone. While you get a lot for that $60, don't kid yourself: it's an Android device without much in the way of guts (http://bkaprt.com/rjs39/01-07).

Moreover, the data presented here illustrates only page speed during *startup*, when critical page assets are downloaded and processed to create the initial user experience. We still grapple with the effects of excessive JavaScript throughout the entire page life cycle—not just during startup.

While it seems like we're quibbling over piddly-sounding things like bytes and milliseconds, every website engages the browser in tons of tasks, including parsing HTML, decoding images, applying styles to said HTML, and—yes—processing and running JavaScript. It quickly adds up.

The result of all that work is a user interface that lets people do stuff, from paying bills to catching up on emails to applying for jobs or government assistance. Your use of JavaScript can either facilitate or impede people in their goals, but you can't know which is the case until you know how the browser schedules and organizes that work on the main thread.

UNDERSTANDING THE MAIN THREAD

Computer processors do their work on *threads*, which are sequences of instructions processed by a scheduler (http://bkaprt.com/rjs39/01-08).

JavaScript is a *single-threaded* language. Consequently, all its work happens sequentially on the *main thread.* This makes the logic linear and easier to follow than that of multithreaded languages, but it also means JavaScript competes for the browser's attention with other types of work.

Let's peek at how a browser might schedule toggling a navigation menu on the main thread. Say that menu has an `id` of `mobile-nav` that gets toggled into an open or closed state by clicking on a button with an `id` of `mobile-nav-btn`. That code might look something like this:

```
document.addEventListener("DOMContentLoaded",
function () {
  const mobileNav = document.getElementById("mobile-nav");
  const mobileNavBtn = document.getElementById("mobile-nav-btn");

  mobileNavBtn.addEventListener("click", function ()
  {
    let nextExpandedState = mobileNavBtn.getAttribute("aria-expanded") === "false";
```

DOMContentLoaded event fires	Mobile Nav Toggled On	Mobile Nav Toggled Off
Event: DOMContentLoaded	Event: click	Event: click
Function Call	Function Call	Function Call

FIG 1.5: A simplified visual representation of work scheduled on the main thread. A DOMContentLoaded event fires, running a callback to wire up mobile navigation toggling behavior. Soon after, the user taps the mobile navigation toggle button once to open, and once again to close the navigation.

```
      mobileNav.classList.toggle("mobile-nav-open");
      mobileNavBtn.setAttribute("aria-expanded",
    nextExpandedState);
    });
  });
```

Assume when this script is loaded, someone plops their finger onto the navigation toggle once to open it and then again to close it. That translates into work that's scheduled on the main thread like so:

1. A callback runs when the document's DOMContentLoaded event fires as the page loads. That callback sets up the navigation toggling behavior.
2. The navigation toggle button is, er, toggled, which triggers the callback to add the mobile-nav-open class on the navigation.
3. The navigation toggle button is toggled again, removing the mobile-nav-class on the navigation.

A simplified visual representation of this work shows that it occurs sequentially on the main thread, with each event's callback invoked as the corresponding events fire (**FIG 1.5**). (This kind of visualization is similar to what would be depicted in a performance profiler, a type of performance assessment tool we'll learn about in Chapter 3.)

By the way, I sort of lied about JavaScript being single-threaded. It's possible to schedule JavaScript activity on other threads using web workers (http://bkaprt.com/rjs39/01-09), which helps keep the main thread from getting too con-

8 RESPONSIBLE JAVASCRIPT

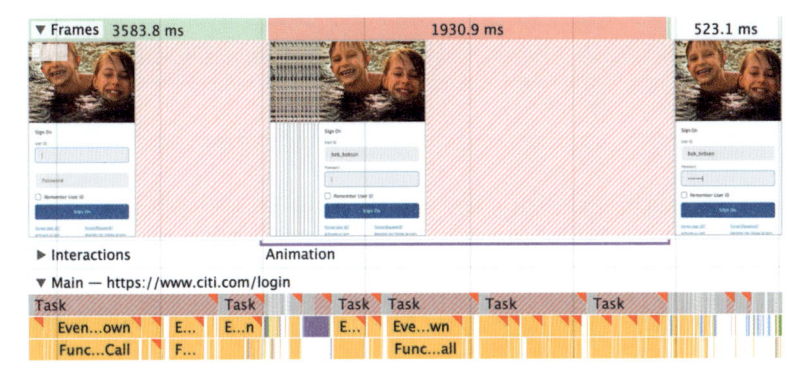

FIG 1.6: A performance profiling session of the login form for Citibank as shown in Chrome's performance profiler. Every keypress triggers excessive main-thread work, resulting in a nearly two-second delay that causes the login form to be unresponsive while entering a password.

---

gested in some situations. But don't get too comfortable with the notion of offloading all kinds of work to separate threads just yet! Web workers, while useful in their time and place, only have direct access to a subset of APIs available to the main thread. We'll touch more on web workers and what they can (and can't) do in Chapter 6.

Frames, tasks, and JavaScript hang-ups

If you understand the main thread as a straight line representing a task queue, you'd be right to also think of that line as representing time. Every task scheduled on the main thread requires some amount of time to complete.

The problem is that the main thread isn't some juggernaut that can take all comers. It has limitations that flex with a device's capabilities and ambient conditions. Schedule too much work on the main thread at once, and it'll get bogged down. When this happens, interactions with a page can't take place until that work is finished (**FIG 1.6**).

Consequences of an overworked main thread vary. A busy main thread can block user interactions with a briefly annoying lag. Worse scenarios can cause the browser to freeze for yawn-

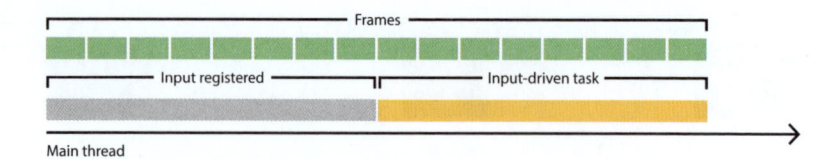

FIG 1.7: The first 50 milliseconds of a task is the budget for the initial user input (e.g., click or tap) to be registered. The task must finish within the remaining 50 milliseconds in order to feel responsive.

---

ing stretches of time, making the page seem broken. Either way, poor runtime performance endangers trust and may frustrate people to the extent that they'll abandon your website.

The threshold at which someone perceives an event as instantaneous is 100 milliseconds (http://bkaprt.com/rjs39/01-10). If a browser is to do everything asked of it seamlessly, with no perceptible performance problems, each task must fit within a *frame*.

A typical display refreshes sixty times per second, making a frame one-sixtieth of a second, or 16.66 milliseconds. But because the browser requires time in each frame for its own processing overhead, the target to complete a task in a frame is 10 milliseconds (http://bkaprt.com/rjs39/01-11).

In practice, you only need to hit the 10-millisecond mark for every frame of an animation or scrolling to be perceptibly smooth. For other work, 50 milliseconds or fewer per task is what you're after. If it takes no more than 50 milliseconds for an input to be registered, and no more than another 50 milliseconds for the browser to respond to that input, that interaction will be perceptibly instantaneous (**FIG 1.7**).

In performance lingo, any task exceeding 50 milliseconds is called a *long task* (http://bkaprt.com/rjs39/01-12). Tasks become long tasks due to the amount of JavaScript activity during any given interaction, including any tangential activity (e.g., layout and paint operations). How fast this work is done is governed by the device it takes place on.

LEFT TO OUR DEVICES

This is where it gets "in the real world" real: the diversity of devices that access the web is *mind-bending*. The spectrum of possible network conditions is similarly wide, and phenomena such as poor coverage areas or congested networks can wreak all sorts of havoc on page performance (http://bkaprt.com/rjs39/01-13).

While one's network connection is an important aspect of web performance, device speed is also important. This is especially true when it comes to whether a page *feels* fast to the person using it.

Thermal throttling: The device performance killer

Every device has a processor, which emits heat as it crunches through tasks. Devices such as desktops and laptops keep processors at a safe operating temperature with a combination of active and passive cooling in the form of a fan and a conductive metal heat sink to absorb and dissipate heat (**FIG 1.8**).

Since mobile-device manufacturers optimize for portability, they ditch fans in favor of passive cooling alone. This leaves devices more susceptible to overheating. To keep those little phones from burning up, processors employ *thermal throttling*, reducing clock speed and power consumption (which in turn reduces device performance) until the excess heat dissipates.

This—as well as a given device's inherent capabilities—contributes significantly to the performance gap between high- and low-end devices. If we can't relegate JavaScript workloads to a manageable amount, we can't guarantee good user experiences across a wider variety of devices.

The device performance gap

People use the web for a slew of tasks where access is of critical importance: online banking, job applications, rental applications, crisis intervention, applying for unemployment assistance, and more. When JavaScript is the first tool we reach for

FIG 1.8: A heat sink / fan combination installed on a processor on a consumer laptop board. Heat sinks absorb and dissipate heat from processors to maintain performance and extend device life. Photograph by Saud (http://bkaprt.com/rjs39/01-14), CC BY-SA 4.0 (http://bkaprt.com/rjs39/01-15), via Wikimedia Commons.

---

to solve every problem, we risk restricting access rather than expanding it.

As an example, I profiled the government of South Carolina's unemployment benefits application website, and measured the impact of its 1.7 megabytes of decompressed JavaScript on startup time across five different devices (**FIG 1.9**):

DEVICE	AVERAGE PROCESSING TIME DURING STARTUP
2017 5K iMac	253 milliseconds
Second generation iPhone SE	301 milliseconds
ASUS X550C Windows 10 laptop	709 milliseconds
Nokia 2 Android Go Edition	6,044 milliseconds
2015 MacBook Pro	621 milliseconds

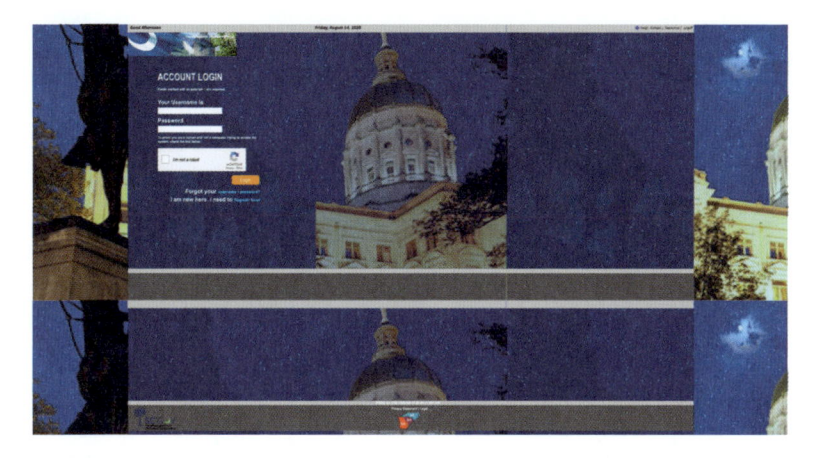

FIG 1.9: As of mid-2020, the government of South Carolina's homepage for unemployment assistance shipped approximately 800 kilobytes of compressed JavaScript, which ultimately decompressed to 1.7 megabytes.

You, being the observant reader you are, will notice that one of those numbers is much bigger than the others. Four out of five of these devices process the JavaScript on this website satisfactorily. Yet one of those devices—the budget device—practically dies trying to do the same amount of work. This disparity represents what I mean by "the device gap" as it pertains to JavaScript performance.

The Nokia 2 is a resource-constrained device. It ships with a quad-core Cortex A7 processor (http://bkaprt.com/rjs39/01-16) and 1 gigabyte of RAM. You can buy a Nokia 2—or a similar device—for less than $100 USD. This price point makes this—and similar devices—a pragmatic choice for many people.

We aren't just concerned with watching funny cat videos here. In 2015, 41 percent of job-seeking Americans used a mobile phone in some part of their job search (http://bkaprt.com/rjs39/01-17). When we ship excessive JavaScript, those who can't spare money for high-end devices face barriers to participating not only in the fun and frivolous things the web has to offer, but in the economy itself.

Human beings are often self-serving creatures, and web developers are no different. It's tempting to rationalize that those on low-end hardware or slow network connections aren't part of your "target audience." Let's recognize that sentiment for what it is: an intentional choice to exclude people.

We must strive to build websites that reach *everyone* while still delivering high-quality experiences through more considered use of JavaScript. Building for the web in this way maximizes your reach—and expands access.

THE WEB IS IN OUR CARE

Internet access not a luxury, but essential to functioning in an interconnected world. This means that we must recognize that our constraints are not static. While we want to use more JavaScript in our work—and we certainly have been—our preference for it as a first resort has consequences.

Networks can only go so fast, and the main thread can only take on so much work. The more JavaScript you send down the pipe, the slower the target device becomes and the faster the promise of usability fades. This breeds frustration that only we can fix.

As we move forward from this chapter, let's abandon our sphexishness and focus on how the web is experienced by real people. Our users are dependent on the critical fixtures the web provides. Now that we have a grip on how JavaScript impacts performance, we can discuss how our architectural choices can help or harm the user experience. As we'll learn, we don't need to rely on JavaScript as the principal driver of interactivity; instead, let's look at its potential as an enhancement.

2 FAST FROM THE START

BEFORE A PAPER WASP FOUNDRESS builds her nest, she first builds a foundational support structure called a *petiole*, a fibrous stalk that supports the entire nest (**FIG 2.1**). A petiole is durable enough to support a nest in all sorts of adverse conditions, even well after a colony has died out. It's a simple, sustainable, and crucial structure that plays a role in the colony's survival.

Just as a paper wasp's nest can't exist without a petiole, no website—regardless of its architectural makeup or how much JavaScript it uses—can exist without a web server. And websites are especially resilient when they rely on the backend to provide markup and functionality first.

Then, like wasps that expand their nests into tiers connected by additional petioles, we can decide when it's appropriate to expand upon our work with frameworks and libraries. This incremental approach restrains the role of JavaScript, ensuring smoother, more resilient user experiences that work in more places.

FIG 2.1: Paper wasp nests are suspended by a foundational structure called a petiole. Photograph by the author.

BRING ONLY WHAT YOU NEED

In our line of work, we're habituated to roll with off-the-shelf solutions that simplify web development. While it's arguably easier to lean on frameworks and libraries, to do so is to subscribe to someone else's vision of how to build for the web. The potential incongruity between their approach and your project's unique requirements may very well invite heavy performance costs and poor user experiences.

The historical role of frameworks and libraries is central to my argument: when tools like Prototype and jQuery rose to prominence, there was a dire need to bridge the gaps between differing implementations of various browser APIs. Thanks to the proliferation of web standards, consistency is much easier to achieve without having to rely on such stopgaps—if only we can break the habit.

Platforms over libraries

One way JavaScript bloat creeps into projects is through the unnecessary inclusion of utility libraries. Lodash is one such library that gained traction during a time when JavaScript itself couldn't conveniently accomplish what Lodash's utility functions could. These days, bare JavaScript can replace some of what Lodash provides.

One use case for Lodash is mapping a function to each member of an array to transform its contents. For example, you could transform an array of URL strings for page assets into markup, then join the results into one string:

```
import _ from "lodash";

  const scripts = ["/js/scripts.js", "/js/vendors.
  js"];
const markupArray = _.map(scripts, script => {
  return '<script src="${script}"><\/script>';
});
const markup = _.join(markupArray, "");
```

While Lodash does this well, this code can be updated to use JavaScript features available in the browser:

```
const scripts = ["/js/scripts.js", "/js/vendors.
  js"];
const markup = scripts.map(script => {
  return '<script src="${script}"><\/script>';
}).join("");
```

Browsers ship enough JavaScript features to let you do damn near anything without utility libraries. For example, you can:

- filter arrays with `Array.prototype.filter` (http://bkaprt.com/rjs39/02-01);
- reduce an array to a single value with `Array.prototype.reduce` (http://bkaprt.com/rjs39/02-02);

- concatenate two arrays with `Array.prototype.concat` (http://bkaprt.com/rjs39/02-03); and
- get an object's keys, values, or both as an array with `Object.keys`, `Object.values`, or `Object.entries`, respectively (http://bkaprt.com/rjs39/02-04).

That's a mere sampler! There are tons of JavaScript methods at your disposal, available in practically every browser in widespread use (http://bkaprt.com/rjs39/02-05). It pays to think critically about what you're trying to achieve and attempt to solve problems with bare JavaScript first, and then resort to utility libraries if that goal becomes untenable.

Beware the bandwagon fallacy

When the developer community is invested in a framework, it feels like the right choice—the *safe* choice. This is the bandwagon fallacy, an alluring force when it comes to assessing client-side frameworks. Even if everyone *is* using it, it still may not be safe from a user-experience perspective. The trick is to know if a given tool is appropriate for the task at hand.

React is a popular JavaScript framework that emphasizes componentization and simplified state management. It was developed by Facebook, and enjoys strong advocacy from a vocal and dedicated userbase. The State of JS 2020 Survey found that 70 percent of their 23,765 respondents use React (http://bkaprt.com/rjs39/02-06). The survey also revealed that:

- 70.8 percent of respondents identified as white;
- 91.1 percent identified as male, 5.8 percent identified as female, and 0.9 percent identified as nonbinary / third gender;
- More than half (52.6 percent) assessed their proficiency in JavaScript at an expert level and just under half rated themselves at either an intermediate (22.7 percent) or advanced (22.3 percent) level. In contrast, only 2.3 percent rated their proficiency at a beginner level.

These results clearly illustrate that an exceedingly vocal segment of white male developers who self-assess their JavaScript skill at above-average levels advocate strongly for React. They also advocate for a developer experience that favors JavaScript-heavy client-side architectures, which are given to poor performance in adverse conditions—something this segment of developers is far less likely to experience themselves, thus reaffirming and reflecting their biases in their work.

Consider that, as performance engineer Tim Kadlec found in his 2020 analysis of JavaScript frameworks, the median of websites using React shipped 40 percent more JavaScript than the median of all websites (http://bkaprt.com/rjs39/02-07).

Similarly, Kadlec also found that websites using React tended to use more device memory than those using other frameworks at most percentiles (http://bkaprt.com/rjs39/02-08). These choices carry consequences to the performance—and, therefore, to the user experience—that we shouldn't be quick to dismiss.

This is a predictable outcome of the bandwagon fallacy. In large corporate development teams, key decision-makers often adopt technologies such as React because it conforms to their expectations of what makes a good developer experience rather than centering the needs of their users.

This is not to say React isn't useful or doesn't have its place, but rather that what works well for Facebook won't work well for every app. This is true of any client-side JavaScript framework. No amount of bandwagoning nullifies that bare fact. We must consider the framework's overhead—that is, the performance cost it incurs to do its job—to avoid inadvertently restricting access rather than expanding it.

Frameworks don't doom us to build shitty websites, but to use them is to accept a certain amount of overhead you can never optimize away. You must step lightly, particularly since the ecosystem of installable plugins and off-the-shelf components available to such architectures can further compound their user-experience problems.

A client-side JavaScript framework's popularity or ease of use doesn't automatically beget a good user experience. They're conveniences for developers first. Well-worn technologies and direct use of web-platform APIs are often a more usercentric starting point.

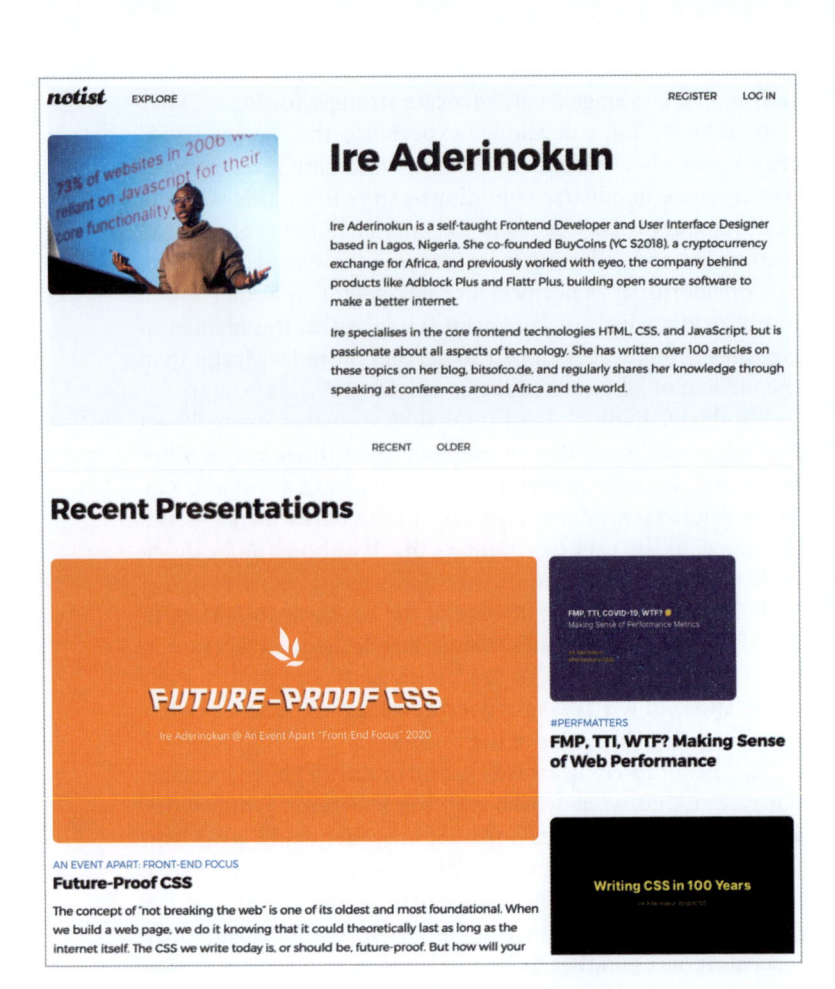

FIG 2.2: Notist is a website for conference speakers that eschews heavy client-side architectures in favor of server-driven functionality by way of a PHP backend with minimal client-side JavaScript.

For example, Notist is a website for conference speakers to showcase their talks (**FIG 2.2**). It runs on PHP and the Apache HTTP Server. While not as attractive for developers accustomed to modern full-stack JavaScript development, it runs on time-tested technologies that have delivered on reliability and speed for decades.

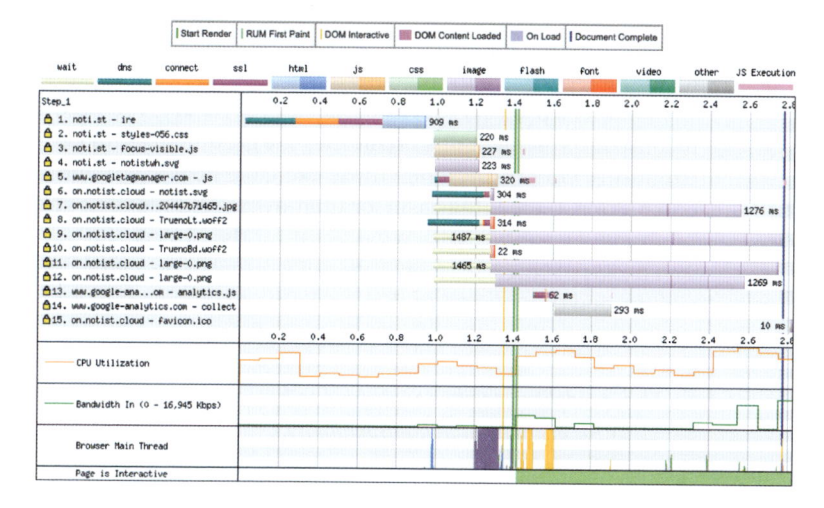

FIG 2.3: A WebPageTest waterfall of a Notist user profile loading on a Moto G4 device powered by a WebPageTest instance in São Paulo, Brazil. The page's largest piece of content paints within 1.5 seconds and is interactive immediately after its first paint.

Notist's architecture also encourages a strong separation of server-side and client-side code. While this can feel like an impediment to productivity, it raises guardrails that guide developers to shipping *less* client-side code. This helps Notist deliver a great user experience that boots quickly with minimal main-thread work incurred by JavaScript (**FIG 2.3**).

Users *do not care* what technologies you use. They only care that a website is fast and accessible. That's the core of what responsible usage of JavaScript is all about: prioritizing user experience over developer experience.

Document your architecture choices

Once you've settled on an architecture that prioritizes a good user experience, drafting a technology statement should be one of your next steps. A *technology statement* is a document that lays out the technology choices for a project and the rationale behind them. It's like a code of conduct, but rather than setting expectations for the behavior of community members, it sets forth the technical requirements for prospective contributors.

Whether a project is open source or proprietary, you need a technology statement that establishes the ground rules for contributions. Otherwise, when those excitable new contributors come along, their enthusiasm for their own preferred tools and methods can conflict with what's best for the project.

The A11Y Project is a comprehensive resource on web accessibility, and this excerpt of their technology statement doesn't mince words about their technology preferences:

> This is a deliberate choice intended to balance:
> - Accessibility and interoperability.
> - Ease of setup.
> - Approachability for beginners.
> - Cross-Operating System and browser support.
> - Local and end-user performance.
>
> When working on the website, please be sure to utilize these technology choices first, and stay with them if at all possible. Honoring these technology choices helps to keep the site easier to maintain. (http://bkaprt.com/rjs39/02-09)

Their statement lists not only the technologies used but also ones to be avoided, and explains why those technologies are incompatible with the A11Y Project's mission to provide an accessible and fast resource on web accessibility. This gives prospective contributors a roadmap to making contributions that align with the project's mission.

Organizations that don't employ a technology statement fail to do so at their own peril, but slapping one into a Git repo or company wiki without much thought isn't much help either. Prominently mention your project's technology statement in a top-level README, with contributing guidelines in a project's repository.

For developers working on proprietary projects for employers, make a technology statement a part of the onboarding process to ensure every participant understands the constraints of the project's architecture. Failing to do so places your project's user experience at risk—proprietary or otherwise.

WHICH SIDE ARE YOU ON?

The first request for any website always involves an HTML response rom the server, but it's really what happens after that initial response that defines the resiliency of what you build—and whether you're providing functionality from the server side or the client side.

Websites vs. web apps

Nomenclature is always tough to navigate. In our industry, terms like *website* and *web app* are flung around without much thought about how they inform our development choices. As this industry grinds away more of my vital life essence, I've come to understand that—while everything we build is *technically* a website—each term is *usually* shorthand for the following:

- A *website* is a collection of pages that provide markup and functionality from the server. Websites tend to treat JavaScript as an enhancement on top of a minimally viable experience.
- A *web app* feels and behaves more like a native app. Web apps treat the server as a data provider that fully relies on client-side JavaScript to provide markup and functionality to create "app-like" experiences.

These distinctions matter because they affect your development style. When you go down the web-app path, you're likely using a package manager (e.g., npm) to add client-side JavaScript in an alluringly frictionless fashion. That kind of convenience can give rise to slow user experiences that raise the bar for access from certain networks and devices, and create unnecessary barriers for users (**FIG 2.4**).

On the opposite side of the spectrum are websites like Self-Defined—a modern dictionary that provides space for people to define aspects of their identity (http://bkaprt.com/rjs39/02-10)—which rely on the server to provide *all* markup and functionality (**FIG 2.5**).

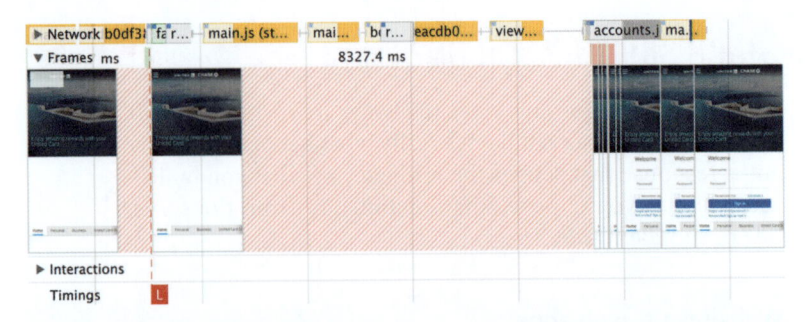

FIG 2.4: A timeline in Chrome's performance profiler of Chase Bank's credit card app login screen, accessed using a budget Android device. While the initial markup is provided by the server, the login form itself (at bottom in the right-hand screenshots) doesn't appear until more than eight seconds later after the page is fully loaded on a slow 3G connection. This is due to requests for multiple JavaScript assets (depicted at top) that are required to render the login form markup on the client.

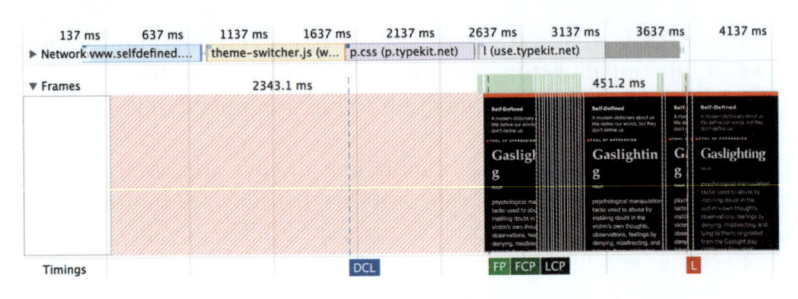

FIG 2.5: A timeline in Chrome's performance profiler of the Self-Defined website, accessed using a budget Android device. Because Self-Defined's markup is served entirely from the server, its core content is available to read almost instantly, even on a slower 3G connection.

Because Self-Defined relies on the server for its crucial markup and functionality, it avoids the unnecessary complexity that comes with building web apps. This allows Self-Defined's maintainers to focus on sharpening its *content* rather than grappling with the ever-changing landscape of frameworks, tools, and best practices often touted alongside them. As a result, it's fast, accessible, and therefore more *inclusive*.

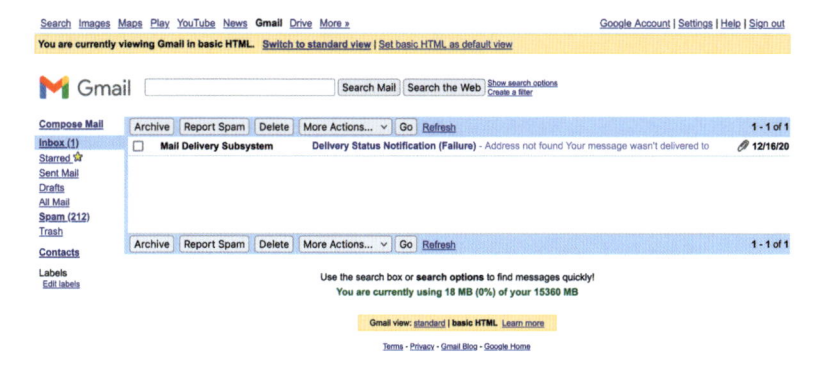

FIG 2.6: Gmail's basic HTML view sends markup from the server and minimal JavaScript in lieu of the JavaScript-heavy client rendering favored by its standard view.

That's not to say that web apps are dirty, awful, no-good things that you should never, ever build in a million years—but be aware that such an approach pulls you down a road that can more easily cause performance issues. Web apps absolutely require client-side JavaScript—and often more of it—by their very nature. If you're going to roll with the web-app model, you have work ahead of you to ensure a good user experience.

Gmail's web app is a prime example of a very heavy client-side web app. It works fine if you have a fast machine and a snappy network connection, since it ships megabytes of compressed JavaScript that decompresses into a hell of a lot more to process and execute. Despite such enormous JavaScript payloads, Gmail sees widespread use. Just in case, though, it allows those on slow connections to opt into a basic HTML view (**FIG 2.6**).

Gmail's basic HTML view uses roughly 50 kilobytes of total data to function, and only a sliver of that is JavaScript. While its appearance is admittedly dated, this stripped-down experience is a server-driven fixture that stands as one hell of an argument that webmail—and other crucial applications—can be functional without being dependent on tons of client-side JavaScript.

That said, you don't have to bifurcate your projects in this way. Nearly every would-be, JavaScript-heavy web app can be made functional with HTML sent from the server and an application backend to handle core functionality. After that, JavaScript becomes the cherry on top of a minimally viable experience.

Server-first is user-first

When someone uses a website, they're interacting with markup. But is it markup sent from the server, or is it rendered on the client by JavaScript? While either approach results in a user interface, they each involve trade-offs.

Let's examine this problem by analyzing how a browser on a budget device deals with markup sent by the server versus markup rendered on the client with JavaScript. For the test case, let's use a Moto E Android 10 device to access Shakespeare's *Hamlet*, with each of its twenty scenes presented on a separate page in unstyled HTML.

There are two different ways to deliver this content: one approach chunks up each scene into its own HTML file, relying on conventional `<a>` elements to navigate between them (**FIG 2.7**). The other approach uses a popular JavaScript framework to render each scene's markup on the client, relying on a client-side router (a tool we'll talk about soon) to navigate between pages (**FIG 2.8**).

This is a highly simplified test case, yes, but it effectively demonstrates the performance penalties incurred by rendering markup on the client. When we send HTML from the server, the browser streams and processes it in manageable chunks, making the work much more efficient than if we delegated it entirely to JavaScript.

When we render markup on the client with JavaScript, we're encapsulating that markup in some fashion within JavaScript, which requires processing on top of loading. After all that business, the browser must execute that script to render the markup. Rendering markup on the client is more expensive by its very nature.

Now let's talk about the real-world effects of client-rendered markup on perceptual performance: web apps that render

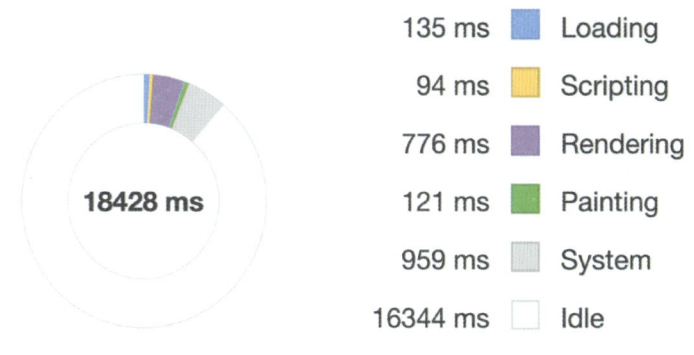

135 ms	🟦	Loading
94 ms	🟨	Scripting
776 ms	🟪	Rendering
121 ms	🟩	Painting
959 ms	⬜	System
16344 ms	⬜	Idle

18428 ms

FIG 2.7: A summary of browser activity when traversing twenty pages presented as separate HTML files using conventional `<a>` elements. The only scripting activity is that incurred by the browser's internals, such as `unload` and `pagehide` event handlers.

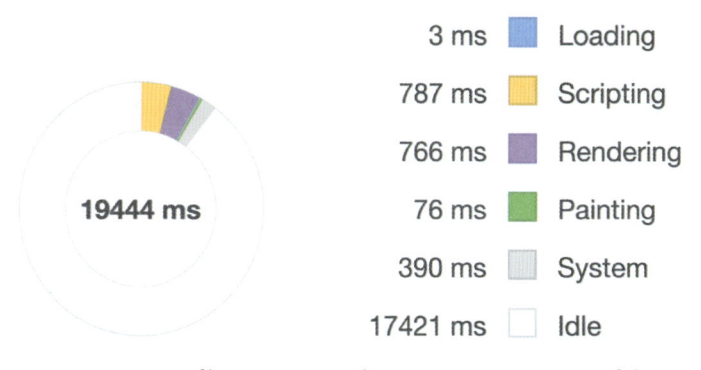

---

3 ms	🟦	Loading
787 ms	🟨	Scripting
766 ms	🟪	Rendering
76 ms	🟩	Painting
390 ms	⬜	System
17421 ms	⬜	Idle

19444 ms

FIG 2.8: A summary of browser activity when traversing twenty pages of client-rendered markup using client-side routing. The scripting activity involved takes more than eight times longer than for the same content presented as separate HTML files.

---

markup on the client often send an *app shell* from the server on startup. An app shell is the minimum amount of markup necessary to bootstrap a web app (**FIG 2.9**). When the scripts requested by the app shell markup load, an API call is made to a server-side API with a `fetch` request.

FAST FROM THE START **27**

FIG 2.9: The app shell for Twitter's mobile web app. The app shell loads immediately, but there's a delay while an API call populates the interface with tweets. A loading indicator spins in the meantime.

FIG 2.10: The Twitter mobile app after a critical JavaScript resource fails to load. The only recourse is to reload the page and hope for the best.

Twitter is a great example of the web-app style of development at work. While Twitter's web app is a reasonably fast client-rendered experience, this model is potentially problematic. When we rely solely on client-side rendering, each script responsible for populating the app shell becomes a potential point of failure (**FIG 2.10**).

Even when all goes well, client-rendered markup can involve a perceptual performance penalty. Those using a client-rendered app must wait not only for the app shell markup but also for API call(s) to populate it with meaningful content (**FIG 2.11**).

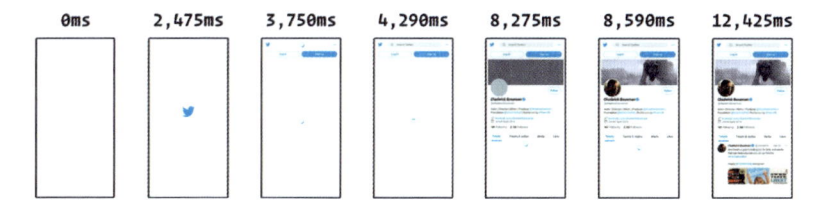

FIG 2.11: A timeline of a Twitter profile loading on a budget Android mobile device on a slow 3G connection. Because the app is rendered on the client, there's a significant delay between the page's first paint and when the page populates with meaningful content.

While client-rendered apps may initially paint very quickly, that paint isn't exactly meaningful.

If, instead, we send contentful markup from the server first and then attach functionality to the interactive parts of the page, we can deliver a more meaningful experience sooner and avoid excluding those with spotty connections or with JavaScript disabled from accessing that content.

Now for some good news! Modern component-based frameworks (e.g., React) can render component markup not only on the client but also on a JavaScript backend as a string. This makes it possible to use the same component code on both the client and the server, which is an improvement for both the user *and* developer experiences.

Don't get complacent, though—server rendering is typically a synchronous and computationally expensive process. You'll need to explore things like component caching in large apps to avoid inflating server response times (http://bkaprt.com/rjs39/02-11).

Whatever technology or application backend you use, the point is that delivering contentful markup from the server provides some semblance of an experience in the potential absence of JavaScript. And—real talk incoming—going server-first is one hell of a starting point for progressively enhancing your website with JavaScript without saddling the client with tons of expensive work.

Client-side routing and accessibility

A common architectural choice for web apps is the *Single-Page Application* (SPA) model, which loads all the HTML from the server up front and then handles subsequent navigations with a JavaScript-powered client-side router that swaps out page contents in an app shell.

SPAs enjoy a perceptual performance benefit in that they avoid the inefficiency of complete page refreshes when navigating to other pages. Aside from the performance penalties of rendering HTML on the client as we've discussed, this approach can pose significant accessibility risks—at least if not done very, very carefully.

Management of navigation and history is governed by a complex specification, and numerous open-source client-side routers have come and gone during its evolution. Not all client-side routers necessarily pay attention to—or may be able to remedy—crucial accessibility issues such as element focus, scroll position restoration, navigation canceling, and so on.

I can't stress enough that when you use a client-side router, you're challenging decades of discovery and foundational work that browser vendors have done to ensure a consistent and resilient navigation experience (http://bkaprt.com/rjs39/02-12).

If you've read this far and still think a client-side router is necessary for your project, consider the following:

- Service-worker technology can increase the perceived speed of navigations by stitching together cached header and footer partials with streamed content partials from the network. Service-worker technology is fast, well supported, and, most important, it's a progressive enhancement of a time-tested and well-established navigation mechanism, not a wholesale replacement of it. We'll cover this approach in detail in Chapter 4.
- If service worker is a no-go and you're dead set on client-side routing, it's crucial that your application backend has a one-to-one relationship with as many client-side routes as possible. This provides access to any part of your website regardless of context—such as through search engine referrals.

- Treat client-side routing as an enhancement. For example, if your website has both authenticated and unauthenticated areas, consider confining client-side routing to only the authenticated portion of your website.

Web developer Marcy Sutton talks about the accessibility impacts of client-side routing at length and has a whole slew of useful recommendations if you insist on it. The one that stands out most to me is this:

> *Consider whether a single-page app is really necessary, and if you even need to use a JavaScript framework at all. (http:// bkaprt.com/rjs39/02-13)*

This advice may seem to fly in the face of best practices. It certainly runs counter to the industry's prevailing JavaScript euphoria, but remember this: a best practice that preserves the developer experience at the expense of the user experience is not a best practice, but rather a self-serving one (http://bkaprt.com/rjs39/02-14).

SENSIBLE CACHING

A section about the browser cache? In a book about JavaScript? Believe it! There's a good reason to bring it up.

The browser cache is an optimization where the server communicates the "freshness" period of assets to the browser. If the browser determines on a return visit to a page that an asset it has on disk is "fresh" according to the server-provided policy, that asset is reused rather than retrieved again from the network (**FIG 2.12**).

The browser cache doesn't do anything for new visitors to your website, but it's a very effective optimization that reduces or eliminates loading time for affected assets on subsequent pageviews. In the case of JavaScript, this means the loading phase is reduced, and the browser can get on with the processing phase more quickly.

	Web Vitals			Fully Loaded		
	Largest Contentful Paint	Cumulative Layout Shift	Total Blocking Time	Time	Requests	Bytes In
First View (Run 1)	3.440s	0.033	≥ 2.204s	10.854s	61	1,281 KB
Repeat View (Run 3)	2.139s	0.007	≥ 2.290s	6.032s	15	90 KB

FIG 2.12: A summary from WebPageTest for a web page on an initial visit (top row) and a repeat visit (bottom row) where caching kicks in. Not only does the return visit transfer 93 percent less data than the initial visit, but its Largest Contentful Paint and Cumulative Layout Shift metrics are improved.

When a browser requests an asset, the response contains HTTP headers that describe its characteristics. Browser caching is affected by a handful of response headers, but the most flexible and commonly used one is `Cache-Control` (http://bkaprt.com/rjs39/02-15).

`Cache-Control` specifies a caching policy composed of one or more directives that describe how an asset should be cached. A common directive is `max-age`, which specifies the number of seconds an asset is valid for. Say you request an HTML document and this header appears in the response:

`Cache-Control: max-age=300`

This says to the browser, "Hey, this asset can be reused for up to three hundred seconds." That's five minutes to us humans.

There's a catch to `Cache-Control` that has to do with whether an asset is cached not just by the browser but also by an intermediate cache such as a *content delivery network* (CDN). A CDN is a proxy in front of your website that distributes assets to edge servers that are physically closer to your website's visitors. Minimizing physical distance reduces latency.

`Cache-Control` implicitly lets both browsers *and* proxies know they may cache assets. This optimization is a benefit in that the asset is served from the CDN's cache even if it isn't in someone's browser cache. In the case of dynamic content—that is, HTML documents—you'll want to prevent this by specifying the `private` directive in addition to `max-age`:

```
Cache-Control: max-age=300, private
```

How you configure `Cache-Control` depends on your application backend or web server configuration. For Apache web servers, the preceding policy can be set for HTML documents in an `.htaccess` file:

```
<FilesMatch "\.html$">
  Header set Cache-Control "max-age=300,
  private"
</FilesMatch>
```

The amount of time you'll want to cache an asset depends on the asset type. JavaScript files are *static assets*, which means they don't change based on who requests the asset or how. Think of stuff like stylesheets, scripts, images, and fonts—things with contents that don't change based on things like cookies. Configuring caching for these assets requires a two-pronged approach:

- The asset must be versioned so future updates to it won't be passed over due to a previous version of it persisting in browser caches.
- The asset must have a `Cache-Control` policy to ensure it will be reused for as long as possible.

Versioning assets is the most involved of the two, as URLs are how browser caches keep track of assets. If a JavaScript file named `scripts.js` is served from `compuglobalhypermega.net`, this asset is not versioned. If someone visits `compuglobalhypermega.net` on Monday and downloads `scripts.js`, and a `max-age` directive specifies a freshness period of one month, the browser will use the copy in its cache when that user visits the site again on Friday—even if a new version of `scripts.js` was published on Wednesday. That's bound to break stuff.

One workaround is to append a query string to the URL when an asset changes: `compuglobalhypermega.net/js/scripts.js` becomes something like `compuglobalhypermega.net/js/scripts.js?v=1`. When the file changes, the query string is incremented to `?v=2`.

FAST FROM THE START

This approach isn't sustainable for anything but the simplest of websites, so it's best to automate versioning. One way would be to compute a hash of the file's contents in your application backend so that the query string updates itself. The following PHP code example shows how to generate a hash of an asset's contents that is then appended to the URL in a `<script>` tag:

```
<?php $fileHash = md5(file_get_contents("./scripts.
  js")); ?>
<script src="/js/scripts.js?v=<?php echo($fileHash);
  ?>"></script>
```

Another versioning method involves using a bundler—a tool we'll talk about in Chapter 5—to compute the hash of its contents at build time and inject it into the asset's file name. The result is a file name that looks like this:

```
scripts.4d3b7eda068fd80bef9ed2f05d52c3df.js
```

Either way works, because it's very likely that your HTML isn't cached (and if it is, it probably shouldn't be). When the HTML is updated, new assets are referenced instead of old ones and are cached separately.

An optimal caching policy is the second part of this soiree. This is an example of a strong caching policy for a versioned static asset:

```
Cache-Control: max-age=31536000, immutable
```

This instructs the browser to cache the associated asset up to one year. We've also added an additional `immutable` directive as a further optimization, which tells supporting browsers, "Hey! This file will *never* change. Don't bother checking with the server to see if it has!"

It may seem weird to cover browser caching in a book about JavaScript, but it plays a big role in the loading performance of many asset types—JavaScript chief among them. That's no small part of using JavaScript responsibly.

PROGRESSIVE ENHANCEMENT

Okay, so you've got server-provided markup and some solid caching practices in place. Now you get to focus on progressively enhancing your website with JavaScript.

Progressive enhancement—as it applies to JavaScript, anyway—is this idea that we first implement a website's essential functionality without JavaScript. Once we have a baseline experience that works without JavaScript, we then apply JavaScript selectively to provide a better experience for those who can benefit from it (http://bkaprt.com/rjs39/02-16).

Progressive enhancement is a hard sell because it requires consensus that an experience should function in more than one ideal way. Yet its chief benefit is that redundant layers of functionality make a website more accessible and inclusive no matter where it's accessed from.

Set a baseline

You can apply progressive enhancement to most critical interaction points. Form-driven interactions are prime examples. For instance, let's take a social media-type website where people can subscribe to new content from other people. This is an excellent example of where we can use progressive enhancement to facilitate a common interaction pattern that we're all familiar with. This functionality is provided by—unsurprisingly—a `<button>` element.

We *could* write some JavaScript to make a `fetch` call to a backend API when that button is clicked, then update its state on the client if the request succeeded. This isn't an antipattern per se, but it shouldn't be the sole way for this functionality to work. It should be an enhancement on top of a server-provided interaction.

To establish that baseline, we'd wrap the Subscribe button in a `<form>` element with an `action` attribute that points to a server route to handle subscription requests:

FAST FROM THE START   35

```
<form method="POST" action="/subscribe">
  <button type="submit" class="subscribe-
  button">Subscribe</button>
  <input type="hidden" name="subscribee-id"
  value="1">
</form>
```

The server ensures that only existing user IDs are valid and that subscription requests can occur only on behalf of the current authenticated user. In short, security guidelines are enforced on the server—even though, yes, the content of the hidden `subscribee-id` input could be modified by some interloper, but to no avail.

Once the server handles the subscription request, the browser is redirected back to the user's profile page. Because the HTML is regenerated for that request, the state provided by the server will then show that the user has subscribed to that profile.

If this interaction seems inefficient compared to a JavaScript `fetch` request, you're not wrong! Thing is, though, the goal at this stage isn't to be efficient but to set a baseline that expands access in the *absence* of JavaScript. There are many causes for why JavaScript may fail to load even when page markup succeeds. If—when—that happens, we can still offer a minimally viable experience.

Enhance!

Okay! We've got ourselves some solid server-provided functionality. Now we can sprinkle on a bit of JavaScript to enhance it.

The Subscribe button's markup is rendered on a JavaScript backend. If we wanted, we *could* use a framework like React on the client-side code to provide the subscribe functionality, and then attach it via JavaScript on the client during startup.

However, using a framework to do this requires us to move with care. Might the performance and accessibility costs be worth it for a better developer experience? Maybe! But this is the time to question the assumption that a good developer experience begets a good user experience.

FIG 2.13: A call stack in Chrome's performance profiler of a click event handled by React to open a mobile navigation menu. React adds a lot of main-thread work for even simple interactions since it must manage component state and changes in the virtual DOM it stores in memory.

Client-side interactions are driven by event listeners. It matters whether you manage event listeners yourself with addEventListener or rely on a framework to handle them, as relying on a framework may incur a high efficiency cost (FIG 2.13).

React's handling of event listeners and their associated state is computationally expensive. Depending on the device, it can sometimes take quite a bit longer for React to do its thing than simple event listeners you'd register yourself—or even a competing framework (http://bkaprt.com/rjs39/02-17).

Remember that any task running longer than fifty milliseconds is a long task; the overhead a framework introduces to manage event listeners gives you a lot less headroom for other work. If we're willing to register event listeners ourselves, we can see that the same interaction is a lot less bulky in terms of processing costs (FIG 2.14).

FAST FROM THE START 37

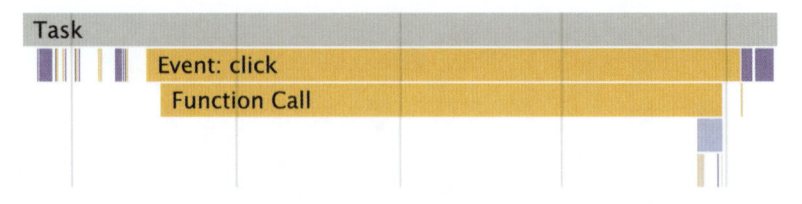

FIG 2.14: A call stack in Chrome's performance profiler of a click event opening a mobile navigation menu without a framework.

While client-side frameworks simplify componentization and state management, you don't necessarily need a framework to manage those things. Web Components may be a viable alternative and more serviceable than you might think.

Web Components aren't a single monolithic web-platform feature but rather a collection of features such as better DOM and CSS encapsulation through shadow DOM, custom elements, and HTML templates. Like component-based frameworks, Web Components offer componentization and the ability to track state in a centralized location.

Before we get into how we might use Web Components, let's revisit the markup for our server-driven Subscribe button from earlier:

```
<form method="POST" action="/subscribe">
  <button type="submit" class="subscribe-
  button">Subscribe</button>
  <input type="hidden" name="subscribee-id"
  value="1">
</form>
```

Custom elements may come to mind when you think of Web Components, which you can use to build an entirely new HTML element, like `<subscribe-button>`, for specific situations. Unfortunately, browsers that don't support custom elements won't be able to fall back on default semantics, which means they'll lose important things like the `<form>` element's server-provided functionality.

38 RESPONSIBLE JAVASCRIPT

That's a bummer. Fortunately, we can preserve those semantics in such cases if we reference our custom element's name in the form's `is` attribute:

```
<form is="subscribe-button" method="POST" data-
  subscribed="false" action="/subscribe">
```

Fair warning: as of this writing, the `is` attribute has no support in Safari, either on macOS or iOS, despite it being a living standard in the HTML specification (http://bkaprt.com/rjs39/02-18). For iOS, that means *all browsers* available on the platform, since Firefox or Chrome are essentially Safari under the hood. The alternatives involve not using Web Components, falling back to the server-provided functionality, or *very carefully* evaluating your framework options to find a solution that prioritizes performance.

Getting back on track: you might wonder why we've decided to attach a custom element named `subscribe-button` to the `<form>` element rather than the `<button>` inside of it. This is an important semantic choice! An accessible and progressively enhanceable Subscribe button is more than the `<button>` element itself: it requires the `<form>` element, and everything within it, to function.

This is one part of what it takes to get a custom element off the ground. We still need to write the component JavaScript, which looks like most JavaScript classes you'd encounter:

```
class SubscribeButton extends HTMLFormElement {
  constructor () {
    super();
  }
}
```

This doesn't seem like an impressive beginning, but there's a lot behind this starter code that makes custom elements so useful in a progressive-enhancement context. Primarily, the `SubscribeButton` class extends the `HTMLFormElement` class. As a result, we retain all the baked-in functionality and accessibility semantics of the `<form>` element for our custom element. All because we decided to extend an existing element rather than create one from scratch (which you often shouldn't have to do).

As with any `class`, we need a `constructor` method. For now, we call the `super` method, which invokes the parent class's `constructor` method. This ensures we gain all the functionality and properties of the `HTMLFormElement` class.

From here, we use the component's `constructor` method to establish the necessary object properties for the Subscribe button to work:

```
class SubscribeButton extends HTMLFormElement {
  constructor () {
    super();

    this.subscribeButton = this.querySelector(".subscribe-button");
    this.subscribed = this.dataset.subscribed === "true";
    this.subscribeeId = Number(this.querySelector("[name='subscribee-id']").value);
    this.buttonLabel = this.subscribed ? "Subscribed" : "Unsubscribe";
    this.coarsePointer = window.matchMedia("(pointer: coarse)").matches;

    // Wire up methods
    this.subscribeButton.addEventListener("mouseenter", this.hoverOn);
    this.subscribeButton.addEventListener("mouseleave", this.hoverOff);
    this.addEventListener("submit", this.subscribe);
  }
}
```

Woof, there's a bit going on there. Let's break down each part:

- `this` refers to the DOM node the web component is attached to. In this case, `this` is the Subscribe button form's `<form>` element.

- Because `this` represents the component instance, we can derive additional scoped properties from it, starting with the `<button>` element within the form itself.
- We can also derive other useful information from `this`, such as the subscription state stored in the `<form>` element's `data-subscribed` attribute, and the subscribee's user ID, the text content of the component's `<button>` child node. We can even store whether the current device has a coarse (touchscreen) or fine (mouse) pointer as a class property.

With these properties, we then wire up event listeners that call class methods providing the following functionality:

- `mouseleave` and `mouseenter` events on the component's `<button>` element for devices with a fine pointer will call the component's `hoverOn` and `hoverOff` methods. Because only those with fine pointing devices (such as a mouse) can "hover" over stuff, we don't want to attach such event listeners for users on touchscreen devices.
- A `submit` event listener on the `<form>` element calls the web component class's `subscribe` method. This method fires a `fetch` request to handle the current authenticated user's subscription request.

Beyond this point, we define each method. Let's start with the hovering methods:

```
class SubscribeButton extends HTMLFormElement {
  // ...

  // Methods
  hoverOn () {
    if (this.subscribed) {
      this.buttonLabel = "Unsubscribe";
      this.subscribeButton.innerText = this.buttonLabel;
    }
  }
```

```
hoverOff () {
  if (this.subscribed) {
    this.buttonLabel = "Subscribed";
    this.subscribeButton.innerText = this.
buttonLabel;
  }
 }
}
```

`hoverOn` and `hoverOff` manage a hover effect if the user is already subscribed to the current profile. In that case, the component's `<button>` element reads "Subscribed," but if a fine pointer hovers over that button, its label will change to read "Unsubscribe."

Next, we define two methods that will enable and disable the component's `<button>` element in certain circumstances:

```
class SubscribeButton extends HTMLFormElement {
  // ...

  disableButton () {
    this.subscribeButton.setAttribute("disabled",
  "disabled");
  }

  enableButton () {
    this.subscribeButton.
  removeAttribute("disabled");
  }
}
```

`disableButton` and `enableButton` will—as their names so boldly suggest—change the `disabled` attribute of the component's `<button>` element. These actions are taken if a `fetch` request is in flight to avoid multiple subscription requests from occurring.

Now for the big method, which sends the `fetch` request:

```
class SubscribeButton extends HTMLFormElement {
  // ...

  subscribe () {
    if ("fetch" in window) {
      event.preventDefault();

      this.disableButton();

      fetch("/api/subscribe", {
        method: "POST",
        body: JSON.stringify({
          subscribeeId: this.subscribeeId
        }),
        headers: {
          "Content-Type": "application/json"
        },
      }).then(response => response.json()).then(data => {
        if (data.state === true) {
          this.enableButton(this.subscribeButton);
          this.subscribed = !this.subscribed;
          this.buttonLabel = this.subscribed ? "Unsubscribe" : "Subscribe";
          this.subscribeButton.innerText = this.buttonLabel;
        }
      }).catch(() => {
        alert("Couldn't subscribe to this person due to a glitch on our end. Try again in a minute?");

        this.enableButton();
      });
    }
  }
}
```

FAST FROM THE START **43**

This method is a busy one, but here's the play-by-play:

1. `event.preventDefault()` is called to keep the form from submitting to the server, which lets the web component handle the subscription functionality.
2. The Subscribe button is disabled.
3. A `fetch` call hits the server with the subscribee ID in a stringified JSON payload as a POST request. From there, the server processes the subscription request.
4. If the request succeeds, the button's text content is updated to reflect that state. Otherwise, a basic `alert` announces that there was a problem. The button is reenabled after the `fetch` call finishes regardless of its success.

That's a wrap! After all that work to try to create a progressively enhanced experience, you couldn't be blamed for wondering what it was all for—but rest assured, the work has a purpose beyond getting a little ol' button to do its thing in the most minimalist way possible.

The rewards of progressive enhancement

When it comes to web development, it can be easier to build functionality solely on the client side than it is to provide that same functionality from the server and then progressively enhance it with JavaScript.

Yet—and I can't be more emphatic when I say this—it *is* worth it. When you go this way, you're doing a hell of a lot to help people out:

- Redundant functionality gives people a safety net in situations where JavaScript is either turned off or fails to load. You cannot control how people visit your website, and progressive enhancement creates a good fallback.
- Progressive enhancement raises guardrails that force you to think more carefully about how you use JavaScript by increasing the role of the server in providing functionality. The end result is a more resilient user experience.

For what it's worth, you don't need Web Components to progressively enhance your website—this was a mere example of how they can be used in pursuit of that goal. But you should begin every project with that same sense of minimalism to set you up for the best outcomes early on, and then layer on flashier tactics should the need arise.

It's only from minimalism that we're going to build a web that relies less on JavaScript when it matters most. If we start with heavy and prescriptive frameworks out the gate, we can't get there. Don't move fast and break things; move thoughtfully and act with care.

GOING FORWARD

It's a hard row to hoe when it comes to building sustainably for the web. But if we prioritize the role of the server in sending markup, employ effective caching, use the web platform when possible, and embrace progressive enhancement, we can avoid shipping costly frameworks to the client, and avoid the potentially expensive overhead they can incur during both startup and runtime.

It may seem like the preferable thing to move as fast as possible—and indeed, it may be, if the goal is to get to market before anyone else—but these choices have consequences beyond the present moment. Your early technology choices may become fossilized into your project, making it exceedingly difficult to remedy the problems they cause down the line. It's one thing to ship code early and often, but it's an entirely different endeavor to deal with the user-hostile consequences of that philosophy.

Sustainable architectures should be about making the web more usable for more people. When architectures expand access rather than inhibit it, we create experiences that are more resilient and fault tolerant. As we continue together, we'll further explore the nooks and crannies of what this good work entails.

3 MEASURING AND ASSESSING JAVASCRIPT PERFORMANCE

IF YOU'VE SPENT ENOUGH TIME OUTDOORS, you know about horseflies. They're dipteran terrors that land on warm-blooded creatures—horse and human alike—and use their scissorlike jaws to feed on blood.

The horse guard wasp kills horseflies, and is a boon to farmers who keep livestock. Even better, livestock aren't at all bothered by the wasps; they accommodate them because their presence is a benefit (**FIG 3.1**).

Using JavaScript responsibly requires a level of vigilance like that of the horse guard wasp, ceaselessly scanning its domain for pesky horseflies. You must keep an eye on JavaScript and restrain its most detrimental effects, as overreliance on it will drag your website's user experience into Slow Town. In this case, vigilance requires measuring and assessing your website's JavaScript situation.

When we *measure* JavaScript performance, we want to know three things:

1. Is the page perceptibly fast and usable during startup?
2. If not, then what's the problem?

FIG 3.1: The horse guard wasp hunts and kills horseflies that pester livestock. Photograph by Howard Ensign Evans, Colorado State University, Bugwood.org (http://bkaprt.com/rjs39/03-01), CC BY 3.0 US (http://bkaprt.com/rjs39/03-02), via Wikimedia Commons.

---

3. Does the main thread quiet down enough after startup so that the page stays usable?

In the same way you can't reliably cut a piece of lumber to the right length without measuring first, we can't assess the impact of JavaScript in our websites and applications until we can measure page performance. That means understanding metrics.

METRICS: YOUR KEY TO MEASURING JAVASCRIPT PERFORMANCE

We all rely on metrics in life. We check the outside temperature to make sure we're properly dressed for the weather. We (hopefully) watch the car's speedometer as we drive to avoid driving recklessly. We use blood panel results to inform our lifestyle choices, such as changing our diet if our triglycerides are too high.

Web performance metrics are similarly essential for making informed decisions. They're also among the many factors that affect how Google ranks pages (http://bkaprt.com/rjs39/03-03). Search engines want to surface the best websites for a given query, and a poor user experience interferes with that goal.

Web performance metrics can be categorized in one of two ways:

- **Lab metrics:** These metrics are gathered by synthetic testing tools such as WebPageTest, Lighthouse, or your browser's developer tools. You can establish consistent baselines with them, which can be useful when you're trying to solve performance problems during development.
- **Field metrics:** These are gathered via in-browser JavaScript APIs from your website's visitors, and then transmitted to a remote data store for later analysis. Field metrics are gold, because they tell the story of how your site's performance is experienced by actual people.

Knowing which metrics are which helps you understand how they apply to your work. Some metrics fall under both categories, while others belong to one or the other. Let's look at some of the most common aspects of page—and JavaScript—performance that metrics can describe.

Painting

Key perceivable milestones that occur during page load are when bits of the page are drawn to the screen. It's the first clue we get that something's happening. Any time a browser draws pixels to the screen, we call that *painting*—and there are a whole bunch of paint metrics out there.

JavaScript's effects on paint metrics often come down to how markup is rendered. Client-side rendering of markup—an expensive process we covered in Chapter 2—can trigger paint events later compared to initial markup sent by the server. This all is magnified by the size of the scripts that render client-side markup, the speed of the network, and how the scripts are delivered.

FIG 3.2: A performance trace in Chrome's performance profiler showing a page's First Paint (FP) and First Contentful Paint (FCP). The FP occurs when the gray background appears, and the FCP occurs when the menu toggle appears.

First Paint and First Contentful Paint

Two common paint metrics you'll encounter are *First Paint* (FP) and *First Contentful Paint* (FCP). FP identifies the first moment *any* pixels are painted to the screen, whereas FCP identifies when content has appeared in the viewport—that is, text, images, a non-white `<canvas>` element, and so on (**FIG 3.2**).

FP is often tied to when a stylesheet loads, but it isn't a terribly important metric. The first thing that paints may not be perceptually meaningful.

FCP, on the other hand, *is* more meaningful in that it's content oriented. The core content of the page might be held up until some beefy JavaScript bundle downloads, is processed, and finally runs, perhaps making a call to a backend API or rendering client-side markup in the process. FCP could well be delayed in that case.

While FCP is an earnest attempt to assess perceptual performance, *contentful* may only describe a background image or an insignificant text node. Thankfully, a more refined metric exists to describe when more prominent content paints.

Largest Contentful Paint

Largest Contentful Paint (LCP) measures the moment when the largest piece of content in the viewport appears—be it an image, video, or text node (**FIG 3.3**). LCP is an improvement over

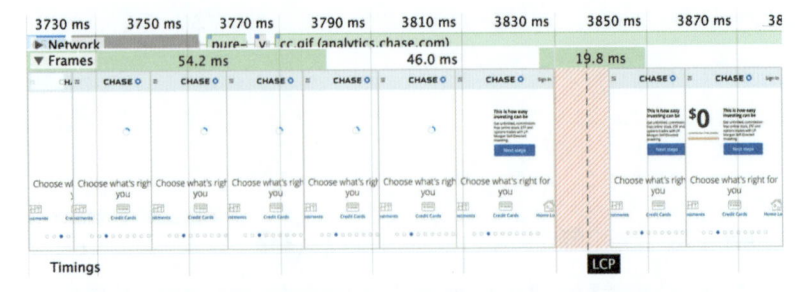

FIG 3.3: A Largest Contentful Paint (LCP) event as shown in Chrome's performance profiler for the Chase Bank website. The LCP is delayed due to client-side rendering of markup for the page masthead.

other paint metrics since it emphasizes content prominence, therefore quantifying more perceptually significant milestones.

As with FCP, JavaScript can interfere with LCP in architectures that rely on JavaScript to render contentful markup on the client. Your website architecture shouldn't require visitors to wait for JavaScript to load, process, and run before prominent content appears on their screens.

Performance-monitoring tools like WebPageTest and Lighthouse report LCP. At the time of writing, Google has advised that an LCP of 2.5 seconds or less is optimal (http://bkaprt.com/rjs39/03-04), but future guidance may vary. The best advice is to shoot for the best possible score, since LCP can affect how your page ranks in search results.

Layout stability

Have you ever gone to click on a link only to have it suddenly move, causing you to click on something else altogether? You're the victim not just of a website's broken promises, but also of *layout instability* (FIG 3.4).

There are many causes of layout instability, and JavaScript is one of them. One example you've almost certainly experienced is when a notice appears at the top of the page late in the page life cycle, pushing the entire layout down. This usually occurs

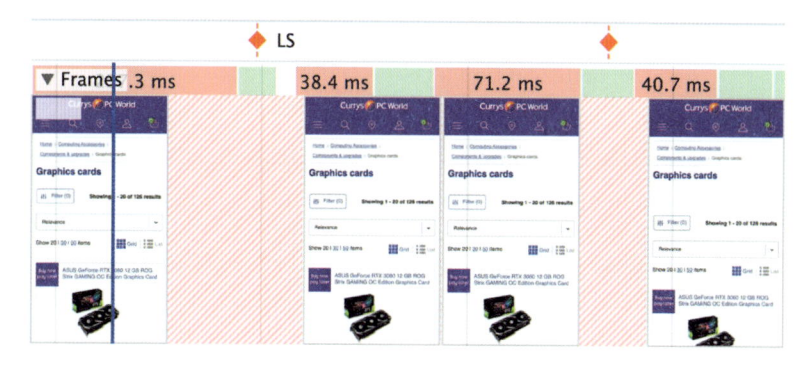

FIG 3.4: As multiple page elements on the Currys PC World website load, the rest of the layout shifts several times, causing key interactive elements to move unpredictably.

because a script takes time to load, process, and run, causing a shift at the worst possible moment.

All layout shifts—whether they're caused by JavaScript or otherwise—cause potentially expensive layout recalculation work that eats up main-thread time. When layout shifts contend for the main thread's attention during startup, we're left with less headroom for JavaScript processing and execution.

It's important to determine whether users can anticipate the layout shifts. Anticipated layout shifts are the result of a voluntary user interaction, such as expanding an accordion. Undesirable layout shifts are those that are seemingly random, without any prior user interaction.

For example, Twitter's mobile website—at least at the time of writing—loads tweets automatically, pushing older tweets down. This causes the infamous "I was about to like a tweet, but now I can't because it's gone" effect. One remedy would be to let the user choose to load new tweets, rather than loading them without any action from the user.

We can measure layout stability with a metric called *Cumulative Layout Shift (CLS)*. Unlike time-based metrics, CLS uses a decimal scoring system that quantifies how far elements have shifted in the viewport from their previous position (http://bkaprt.com/rjs39/03-05). A good CLS score is 0.1 or less, but this could always change as some user-experience metrics may

MEASURING AND ASSESSING JAVASCRIPT PERFORMANCE 51

evolve over time. In practice, the closer you can get this metric to 0, the better off you'll be.

Main-thread responsiveness metrics

JavaScript has considerable potential to delay page startup and interactions. We can assess its impact on the user experience with three metrics: Time to Interactive (TTI), First Input Delay (FID), and Total Blocking Time (TBT)—all of which have significant interplay with one another and with FCP (**FIG 3.5**).

Time to Interactive

Remember that prank where you'd set someone's desktop background to a screenshot of their desktop? Then you'd laugh because your confused victim didn't know they were clicking on a flat image? This is essentially what happens when we delay page startup by shipping too much JavaScript, only we're pranking our users—and in the service of our employers or clients, no less.

Websites that rely heavily on JavaScript tend to have a gap after FCP and before a page and its interface elements are interactive (**FIG 3.5**). This gap has been informally described as "the uncanny valley" of frontend performance—it's not a website yet, but it looks an awful lot like one (http://bkaprt.com/rjs39/03-06).

This effect is prolonged by in-flight network requests for scripts that provide interactivity as well as evaluation of scripts and the long tasks they may incur. The more a website relies on JavaScript, the more likely the uncanny valley will become a canyon.

Time to Interactive (TTI) is a lab metric that measures when a page is interactive. It's calculated by first marking the page's FCP. From there, the next five-second period in which there is neither a long task nor more than two in-flight network requests is also marked. The page's TTI is at the start of that quiet window.

Sites with a high TTI will behave more like screenshots of a website than an actual website, making users think your

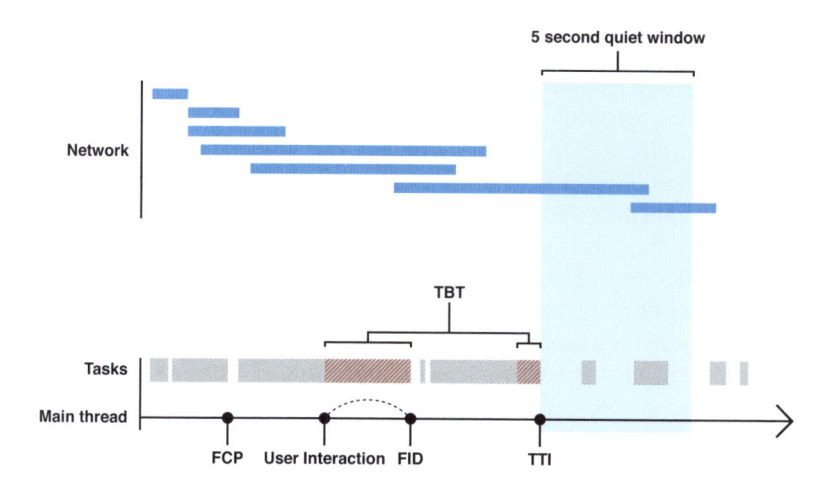

FIG 3.5: Metrics such as FCP, TBT, FID, and TTI are plotted on the main thread, complete with tasks. Refer to this diagram as needed to visualize the page life cycle as we explore each metric.

---

website is busted. A good TTI is less than five seconds on a middle-tier device (http://bkaprt.com/rjs39/03-07), but at the risk of repeating myself, I am once again asking you to aim as low as possible.

First Input Delay

While TTI is great, it describes whether a page is interactive, not whether that page will respond to the first input quickly. *First Input Delay (FID)* is a field metric that fills in this information gap by measuring the delay between the first interaction with a page and when the browser responds to that interaction.

FID isn't strictly a JavaScript metric. Interactions that don't rely on JavaScript (links, form controls, and so forth) still factor into the metric's calculation. If you rely significantly on JavaScript to drive interactivity, however, FID may well reflect that.

FID seems simplistic at first glance, but identifying the cause behind a high FID score gets tough. The first interaction with a page will vary from person to person. Someone on a fast device may present with a high FID score because of excessive

---

MEASURING AND ASSESSING JAVASCRIPT PERFORMANCE 53

JavaScript activity, while someone on the same page with a slow device may show a low FID score because they interacted with the page while the main thread was quiet.

One way to troubleshoot high FID values is to contextualize them so that you know what's happening at the time of the input delay. You can record long tasks from the Long Task API (http://bkaprt.com/rjs39/03-08) occurring around the time of the FID itself. This is what I've done in a small metrics collection script I built (http://bkaprt.com/rjs39/03-09).

Being a field metric, FID yields a wide range of values, so it's sensible to focus on the 95th percentile of those values (http://bkaprt.com/rjs39/03-10). This strategy prioritizes those experiencing extreme input latency.

Total Blocking Time

While TTI and FID are all fine and good, they don't measure the *total* amount of time the main thread is too busy to take on more work during startup. This is where *Total Blocking Time (TBT)* comes in—a lab metric that measures the window of time between a page's FCP and TTI. Where TTI and FID measure distinct points in time, TBT looks at the total blocking time of all the long tasks in that window.

To recap, a *long task* is any JavaScript activity exceeding 50 milliseconds. The *blocking time* of a long task is calculated by subtracting 50 milliseconds from the total time (**FIG 3.6**). If a long task runs for 127 milliseconds, its blocking time is 77 milliseconds.

This means that TBT doesn't penalize *all* JavaScript activity—just *excessive* activity. If your site performs many tasks less than or equal to 50 milliseconds during startup, your TBT score would be zero. TBT also gives vital context for poor TTI scores.

A good TBT score is 300 milliseconds or less on average mobile hardware (http://bkaprt.com/rjs39/03-11). Again, shoot for the lowest score possible. Always measure TBT in synthetic testing tools that use low- to mid-tier devices or CPU throttling, and avoid testing on fast devices. WebPageTest runs its tests on one of a broad range of physical devices in different locations, and reports TBT in its results summary (**FIG 3.7**).

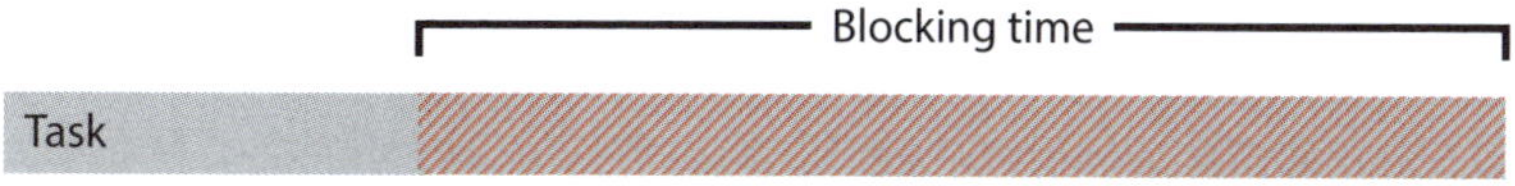

```
┌─────────── Blocking time ───────────┐
Task  ▓▓▓▓▓▓▓▓▓▓▓▓▓▓▓▓▓▓▓▓▓▓▓▓▓▓▓▓▓▓▓▓▓▓
```

FIG 3.6: The blocking time of a long task, illustrated. Blocking time is the long task's length minus 50 milliseconds.

Web Vitals		
Largest Contentful Paint	Cumulative Layout Shift	Total Blocking Time
9.218s	0.618	0.704s

FIG 3.7: WebPageTest's Web Vitals summary includes TBT, as well as LCP and CLS.

You're probably left wondering what you can do specifically to improve your website's performance metrics. Before we can go down that long road, we'll need to look at performance profilers so you can learn how to find specific opportunities for improvement.

PERFORMANCE PROFILERS

Synthetic tools excel at tidily summarizing your site's JavaScript performance. They derive those summaries from data provided by a *performance profiler*—a developer tool that monitors and records all activity (JavaScript or otherwise) that occurs on a page.

Performance profilers exist in all modern developer tools. No matter which browser's performance profiler you use, the goal is the same: you want deep insight into your website's performance so you can find specific opportunities for improvement.

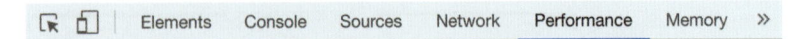

| ▸ ▫ | Elements Console Sources Network **Performance** Memory »

FIG 3.8: An array of tabs at the top of Chrome's developer tools. The Performance tab opens Chrome's performance profiler.

Modern browsers are largely consistent in where they place their performance profilers. To start, open your browser's developer tools and look for the array of tabs across the top (FIG 3.8). Generally, a browser's performance profiler will reside under a tab labeled "Performance" or "Timeline."

Making sense of a populated performance profiler

In its initial state, the profiler's interface will be unpopulated. You'll populate it with data by recording one of two kinds of activity:

1. **Startup activity**. This is all activity that occurs during startup, from the time a page begins loading until somewhat after the `window`'s `onload` event fires.
2. **Specific activity**. You can record any specific time period in order to profile the performance of a given action, such as toggling a menu or validating a form.

All performance profilers provide controls for recording activity. No matter what type of activity you record, the same thing happens once recording stops: the profiler populates with the data from the observation period.

The first time you see a populated performance profiler can feel like being handed the operations manual for a Boeing 737 and being told, "Cool, now take off." Luckily for you, understanding a performance profiler isn't quite as daunting once you grasp a few concepts behind its organization. In fact, you already do!

You'll recall from Chapter 1 that browsers schedule their activity as tasks, and tasks occur within frames. Frames and tasks occur on the main thread, which profilers visualize as a linear progression of time.

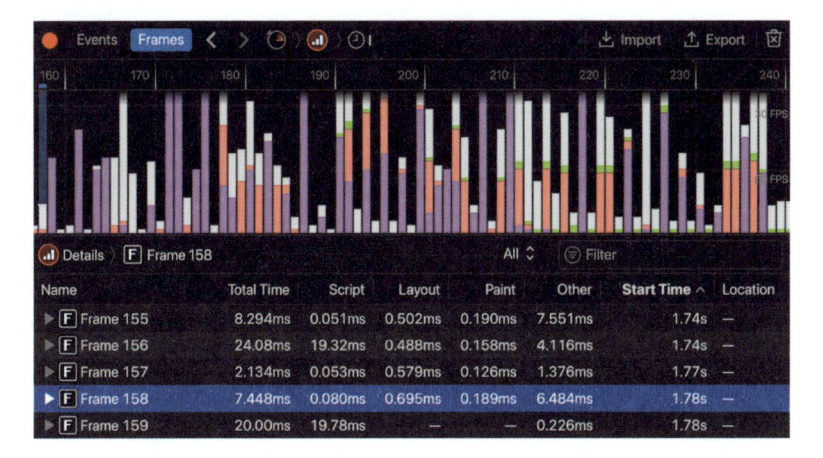

FIG 3.9: In Safari's performance profiler, frames are represented in a bar chart; longer frames are taller bars. The activity in the selected portion is listed in a table below the chart.

Different browsers present this information differently, yet still reflect the task/frame hierarchy. Safari plots tasks sequentially on a line or in a list of call stacks. Safari also offers the ability to view a frame-by-frame accounting of tasks (**FIG 3.9**).

Chrome's profiler takes a hybrid approach. It depicts individual frames, but tasks are displayed as an inverted flame chart (**FIG 3.10**). A *flame chart* is a representation of JavaScript call stacks where each task's call stack is visualized to resemble a literal flame. The base of the "flame" is the task's initiator, with each nested piece of activity stacked below the activity that invoked it.

Because a summary of any giant blob of data is helpful, most profilers provide an overview of all main-thread activity (**FIG 3.11**). A performance profiler's activity overview is interactive, which means you can click and drag to select a range of time, and the flame chart or task list will expand or contract to the selected time period.

Chrome's profiler adds a bottom pane to the flame chart, with tabs that offer filtering controls to surface tasks by duration, type, and name (**FIG 3.12**) as well as a summary of where all CPU time was spent during the observation period.

MEASURING AND ASSESSING JAVASCRIPT PERFORMANCE

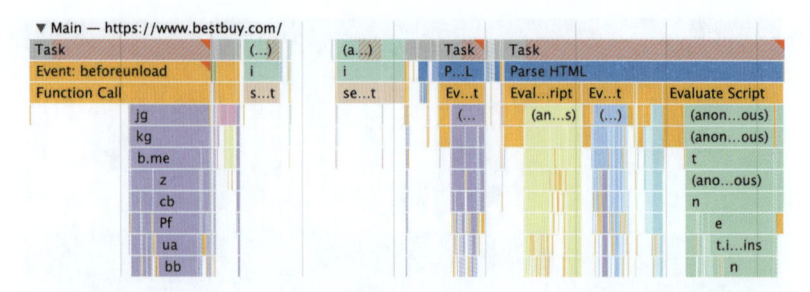

FIG 3.10: A visualization of main-thread activity in Chrome's performance profiler, showing all page activity as an inverted flame chart.

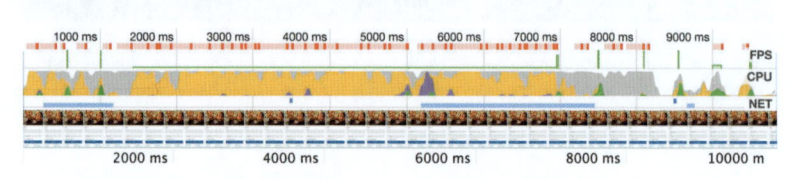

FIG 3.11: The activity overview of Chrome's performance profiler.

FIG 3.12: The bottom pane of Chrome's performance profiler. This pane has several tabs to display summary data as well as detailed lists of page activity.

My own opinion is that Chrome's profiler offers the best combination of usability and depth of information, but use whatever profiler suits you best. The most important thing is that your choice of profiler should help you find opportunities for improvement—and that starts with knowing how to use the profiler to assess loading and runtime performance.

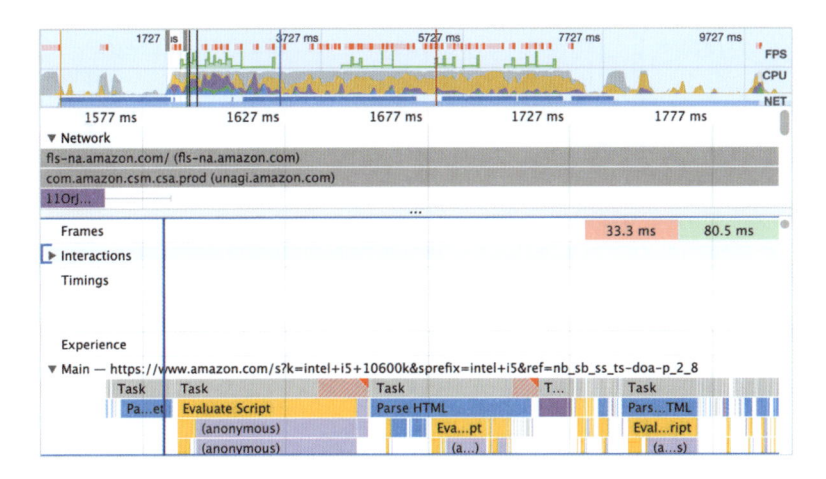

FIG 3.13: A populated view of Chrome's performance profiler for an Amazon product detail page. At the top is the populated activity overview. At the bottom is the flame chart, which shows all the call stacks for the page.

Assessing loading performance

When you assess loading performance, you're telling the profiler to reload the current page and record everything that happens up until the network and main thread are reasonably quiet. Performance profilers in most browsers provide this type of functionality, which gives insight into what happens during the startup phase of any given page (FIG 3.13).

Like so many "whoa, hold up"-type signals you encounter daily, the color red has special significance in Chrome's profiler in that it calls out performance issues. An easy shortcut for finding problems is to scan the profiler's activity overview and look for red strips. These strips represent periods of blocking time—and as we've established, blocking time equals an overworked main thread.

Drill down to problem areas by clicking and dragging across the red strips in the activity overview (FIG 3.14). Because the flame chart expands or contracts to the selection, we gain greater visibility into what's happening at that point in time.

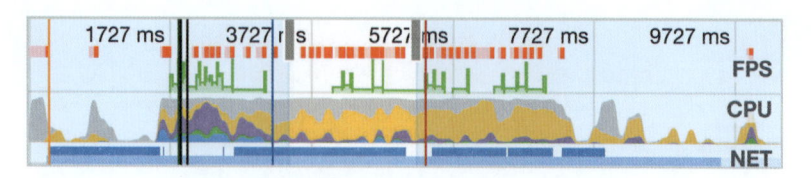

FIG 3.14: The activity overview in Chrome's performance profiler, with a small portion of activity selected. The red strips across the top illustrate periods of blocking time.

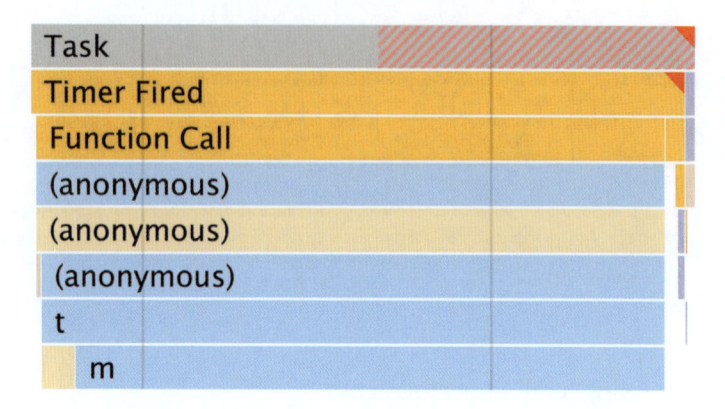

FIG 3.15: A long task—which is at the top of the hierarchy in this view—has a red triangle in its upper-right corner. The blocking portion of the task is marked with red diagonal stripes.

All tasks are displayed in gray, but long tasks display a red triangle in the upper-right corner. Additionally, the blocking portion of the task—that is, the portion exceeding fifty milliseconds—bears red diagonal stripes (**FIG 3.15**).

Call stacks aren't just static visualizations in Chrome's profiler; they're also interactive interface elements. If you're feeling nosy, click on any of the rectangles in a call stack, and a summary of that activity will show up in a pane at the bottom of the profiler window (**FIG 3.16**).

The important bit in the summary view is the file name of the script associated with the selected task. When it comes to script evaluation, we want to figure out what script is rais-

■ Evaluate Script

Total Time 1.48 s

Self Time 0.99 ms

Script www.bestbuy.com/~assets/bby/_js/ext/optmzly/8143030612.js:1

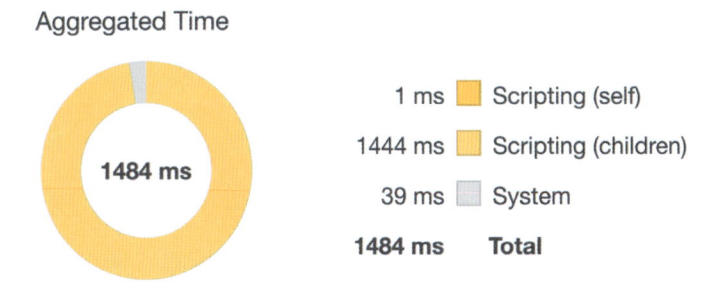

Aggregated Time

1484 ms

1 ms	■	Scripting (self)
1444 ms	■	Scripting (children)
39 ms	■	System
1484 ms		**Total**

FIG 3.16: The summary view shows the task's duration, the task's initiating script, and a breakdown of the task's activity.

---

ing hell, and when we find it, we want to know what we can do about it.

Chrome's coverage tool is useful in this endeavor, as it identifies unused parts of scripts based on the activity it monitors. It's also not immediately visible from the main developer menu; you must press the escape key to open the bottom drawer in Chrome's developer tools, where the coverage tool is squirreled away in a submenu along with other tools.

Like Chrome's performance profiler, the initial state of its coverage tool is empty and must be populated by recording. As it records, the coverage tool will reload the page, then populate a table with information as it's received. The tool continues recording until you stop it.

The first table columns contain the URL to the asset and its type (e.g., CSS, JS, etc.). Subsequent columns detail the used and unused portions of that asset's code (FIG 3.17).

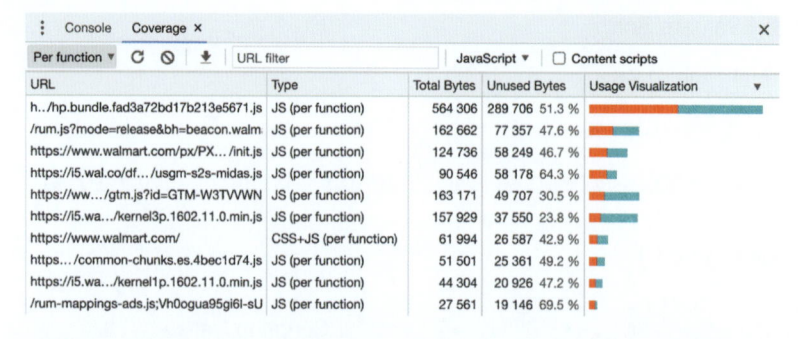

URL	Type	Total Bytes	Unused Bytes	Usage Visualization
h.../hp.bundle.fad3a72bd17b213e5671.js	JS (per function)	564 306	289 706 51.3 %	
/rum.js?mode=release&bh=beacon.walm	JS (per function)	162 662	77 357 47.6 %	
https://www.walmart.com/px/PX.../init.js	JS (per function)	124 736	58 249 46.7 %	
https://i5.wal.co/df.../usgm-s2s-midas.js	JS (per function)	90 546	58 178 64.3 %	
https://ww.../gtm.js?id=GTM-W3TVVWN	JS (per function)	163 171	49 707 30.5 %	
https://i5.wa.../kernel3p.1602.11.0.min.js	JS (per function)	157 929	37 550 23.8 %	
https://www.walmart.com/	CSS+JS (per function)	61 994	26 587 42.9 %	
https.../common-chunks.es.4bec1d74.js	JS (per function)	51 501	25 361 49.2 %	
https://i5.wa.../kernel1p.1602.11.0.min.js	JS (per function)	44 304	20 926 47.2 %	
/rum-mappings-ads.js;Vh0ogua95gi6l-sU	JS (per function)	27 561	19 146 69.5 %	

FIG 3.17: Red indicates the unused portion of each asset, and blue indicates the used portion.

Unused JavaScript is attributable to one or two possibilities:

- The code wasn't executed while the coverage tool was recording. The coverage tool only monitors JavaScript activity that occurs during recording. Interacting with the page during recording may invoke more portions of the script, reducing the reportedly unused portion.
- *Unreachable code*, or code that can never be executed and therefore has no significance (http://bkaprt.com/rjs39/03-12).

Either way, the coverage tool lets you see the unused parts of an asset by double-clicking the asset URL in the table. This opens the asset in an interface like a text editor's. In this view, the unused lines of code are marked with a red marker in the left gutter (**FIG 3.18**).

Some JavaScript engines try to optimize their way around unused code. Chrome's V8 JavaScript engine uses a technique called *lazy parsing* to speed up evaluation of JavaScript at startup, and then compile unused portions of code on demand (http://bkaprt.com/rjs39/03-13). While these optimizations are helpful, they're out of your control, and your users would be better served by splitting the unexecuted code into separate files to be loaded on demand later. We'll talk about this technique in Chapter 4.

```
hp.bundle.fad3a...1.js:formatted  ×

 1   !function(e) {
 2       function t(t) {
 3           for (var n, a, o = t[0], i = t[1], l = 0, s = []; l <
 4               a = o[l],
 5               Object.prototype.hasOwnProperty.call(r, a) && r[a
 6               r[a] = 0;
 7           for (n in i)
 8               Object.prototype.hasOwnProperty.call(i, n) && (e[
 9           for (u && u(t); s.length; )
10               s.shift()()
11       }
12       var n = {}
13         , r = {
14           3: 0
15       };
16       function a(t) {
17           if (n[t])
```

FIG 3.18: When examining a JavaScript asset in Chrome's coverage tool, the unused portions are marked with red in the left gutter. These unused portions of code can be deleted (if they're unreachable) or split out into separate files to be loaded on demand to reduce startup time.

Assessing runtime performance

To recap from Chapter 1, runtime performance describes how responsive a page is to user interactions. Snappy is good, sluggish is bad, and profilers can help you figure out where specific interactions fall in that range of outcomes.

Assessing runtime performance involves profiling a specific activity, which means you'll interact with the page during the recording. Start with interactions that seem sluggish or that serve as a prominent gateway to other parts of the website, so you can prioritize your optimizations.

To profile interactions, first allow the page to completely load. Click the record button in the profiler, perform your chosen interaction (such as toggling a menu), and end the recording. When the profiler populates, it will include the call stack(s) for the recorded interactions (**FIG 3.19**).

From here, you can dive into the recorded interaction by clicking on parts of the call stack, just as you would when you profile startup performance. You'll have access to information

Task							
	Event: click						Up...e
	$t						
	Le						
	Go						
	t.unstable_runWithPriority						
	Xt						
	Zt						
	Xr						
	Function Call						
	(...)	ps					
	le	_s	_s	xs			
	(...)	Es	Es	Go			
	Tr	Os	Os	t.unstable_runWithPriority			

FIG 3.19: Toggling the settings menu on the Target website kicks off a 490-millisecond-long task. The task's blocking time consists of about 90 percent of the total task time, which is considerable for such a high-value interaction.

---

that tells you exactly what kicked off the interaction, and how much time it took. But beware: if you're debugging the runtime performance of interactions on a production website, you'll need to make sure that you're shipping source maps alongside your JavaScript files to aid in debugging (http://bkaprt.com/rjs39/03-14). Otherwise, it may make more sense to profile interactions in a local development build where code is not minified and therefore more readable.

It may seem like a rote exercise to poke and prod at various interactions to see whether they're fast enough, but if you want a bit more precision (and can expend a bit more effort) you might rely on the User Timing API to surface slow interactions with application-specific timestamps (http://bkaprt.com/rjs39/03-15).

Making a website as fast as it can possibly be in all the places it needs to be is a lot of work. If you want to make this work really count, though, take care to measure your website's JavaScript performance on low-end devices to surface potential performance issues more easily—which is just what you're about to learn!

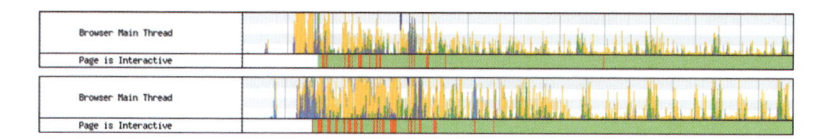

FIG 3.20: At the top is the main thread for a Moto G6 Android phone, and at the bottom is an Alcatel 1X Android phone. The Alcatel 1X incurs more blocking time due to its inferior processing power.

Testing on devices

In Chapter 1, we touched on how performance varies not only across networks, but also across devices. We can observe this in a synthetic testing tool such as WebPageTest, which allows you to run tests on a specific device to assess performance from that device's perspective. This provides access on its results page to main-thread activity visualizations representing different device performance characteristics (FIG 3.20).

While WebPageTest is great for spot checks, it hits a wall when used during development. First, WebPageTest can only reach publicly accessible URLs. Second, it takes a nontrivial amount of time for it to do its thing. These limitations are a real pain when you need to quickly test and retest how code changes affect performance for low-end devices.

A better alternative for local testing is Chrome's remote-device debugging tool, which spins up a developer-tools instance for an Android device connected to a laptop or desktop. If the connected device has USB debugging enabled (http://bkaprt.com/rjs39/03-16), you can access any pages the device has open in Chrome on the host machine's developer tools by pointing Chrome to chrome://inspect#devices (FIG 3.21).

You can launch an instance of Chrome's developer tools from the debugging tool's home screen by clicking on the Inspect link for a page. From there, you can use Chrome's performance profiler to record page activity as you normally would (FIG 3.22).

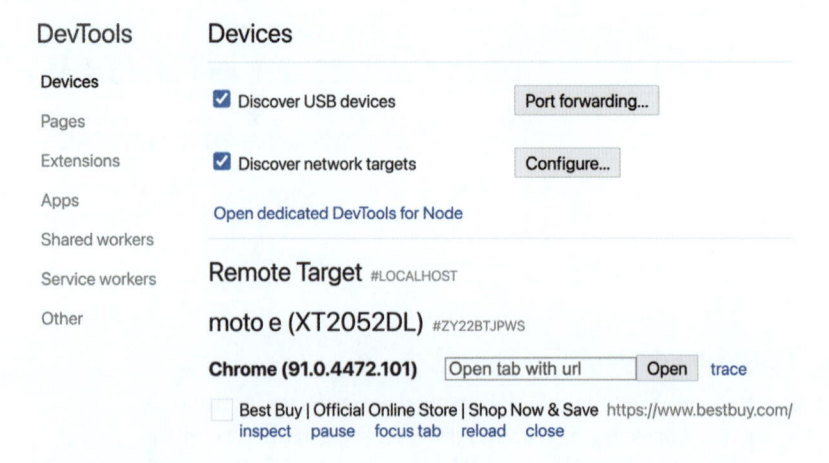

FIG 3.21: The gateway to Chrome's remote-device debugging tool. When an Android device with USB debugging is enabled and pages are open in its Chrome instance, its active tabs will be listed.

FIG 3.22: You can use Chrome's performance profiler to record the activity of the connected Android device; it even shows the device's display contents alongside the profiler.

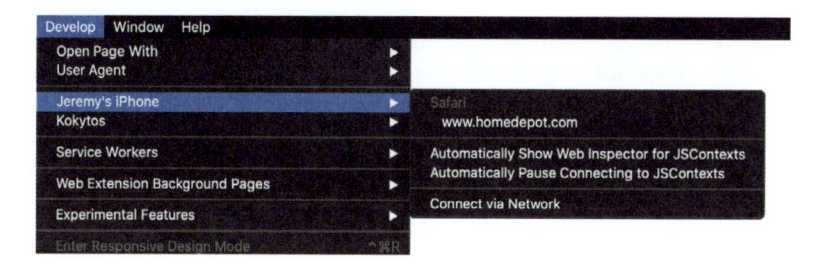

FIG 3.23: Safari's remote-device debugging gateway allows remote debugging of iOS devices connected to a macOS host.

This is, as one might say, a big deal, because it completely changes your profiling context. Chances are that your development machine is beefier than most devices people browse the internet with. When you use Chrome's profiler on resource-constrained devices, you surface issues that would otherwise look a-okay on a decked-out laptop.

Chrome won't let you do this with a connected iOS device, but Safari will if you're on a macOS host with developer tools enabled (http://bkaprt.com/rjs39/03-17). Hook up an iOS device to a macOS host, and you can inspect pages open in Safari via the Develop menu on the host machine. The name of the connected iOS device will appear as its own menu option, with a list of open pages beneath it (FIG 3.23). Clicking on the page URL will launch a Safari developer-tools instance, including the performance profiler.

While this is useful, it's time for some real talk: in April 2021, StatCounter Global Stats found that 41.6 percent of devices it surveyed worldwide were Android devices, whereas just 16.07 percent were iOS (http://bkaprt.com/rjs39/03-18). iOS devices are almost exclusively high-performance devices, while Android devices run the full gamut in terms of performance. Profiling performance on iOS devices just won't surface as many performance issues as profiling performance on low-end Android devices.

If you're uncertain about what devices to profile, test with older, less capable hardware. You'll find more issues, yes, but fixing those issues confers a benefit to all, not the relatively affluent few who can afford high-end hardware. You want to get some visibility into how your website's JavaScript is damaging the trust of your website's visitors regardless of their affluence. That's what responsible practitioners of web development do.

PROFILING JAVASCRIPT PERFORMANCE FOR REAL USERS

So, we've had a bit of talk about lab metrics, field metrics, and profiling performance. The truth is, most of what we've been jawing about amounts to synthetic performance testing, which runs some performance assessment from your local machine using Lighthouse, a performance profiler, or—if you're fancy—tools like WebPageTest that run performance tests from a consistent baseline. When you use these tools, you're gathering lab metrics.

Lab data is great for benchmarking performance improvements from the developer's perspective. You test and uncover a problem with, say, a huge JavaScript asset that's tanking startup performance. You optimize some things, test again, and note changes in your lab metrics. Useful stuff.

Unfortunately, lab metrics only describe one person's perspective: whoever's running the synthetic test. If you want to get a real sense of how your website is performing for actual people out in the world, you need to collect and analyze field metrics.

Gathering field metrics

When it comes to gathering field metrics for later analysis, there are plenty of tools that vary in cost, features, and quality. Collection tools will always require some client-side JavaScript to gather the data from browser APIs and send it to a collection endpoint. There are open-source options that can help you gather this data—such as Boomerang (http://bkaprt.com/rjs39/03-19)—or you can do it yourself.

If you need to collect only a handful of core metrics, something small and simple will do the trick. For my own projects, I wrote a custom solution named `grab-vitals` (http://bkaprt.com/rjs39/03-20), which uses Google's `web-vitals` npm package to gather the performance metrics we discussed earlier:

```
window.addEventListener("load", () => {
  import("grab-vitals").then(({ grabVitals }) => {
    grabVitals("https://interslice.
    compuhyperglobalmega.net/collect");
  });
});
```

The `grabVitals` function accepts a string pointing to a URL where a page's performance metrics will be sent as a JSON string for collection. To avoid contention on the main thread during startup, the `grabVitals` method isn't called until the page `load` event fires.

If you decide to roll your own solution, keep the following in mind:

- Google's `web-vitals` package can't gather all metrics in all browsers without polyfills. That means loading it on some browsers may end up in unused code. `grab-vitals` gets around this by using dynamic `import`—a code-splitting technique we'll cover in Chapter 4.
- Use `requestIdleCallback` (http://bkaprt.com/rjs39/03-21) to avoid main-thread contention with critical interactions. No critical interaction should ever take a back seat to collecting metrics. This API is covered in Chapter 6.
- There are considerable challenges involved with batching collected metrics to avoid excessive calls to the collection endpoint. `grab-vitals` compensates for this by listening for the page's `visibilitychange` event as well as the `pagehide` event for Safari (http://bkaprt.com/rjs39/03-22).

- You'll have to decide whether it's best to send field metrics to your collection endpoint with `fetch` or `navigator.sendBeacon` (http://bkaprt.com/rjs39/03-23). `navigator.sendBeacon` is less complex to use than `fetch` and doesn't delay navigations by delaying document unloading, but `fetch` offers better control.

This stuff is hard! It's not always a bad idea to reach for something off the shelf, even if it's a paid product. Just know that if you decide to work with a vendor to collect field data, you should ask questions to ensure their collection methods address the aforementioned issues.

As far as storing metrics goes, that requires an application backend and a database (http://bkaprt.com/rjs39/03-24). How you store metrics doesn't matter so long as they're accessible to you in a way that's comfortable and familiar.

Tips for analyzing field metrics

Whether you're leaning on a vendor product to gather metrics or rolling your own solution, there are a few things to consider when you analyze the field metrics in your data store:

- **Avoid averages!** While averages are easy to calculate, they don't explain performance the way you think they do (http://bkaprt.com/rjs39/03-25). Averages tend to be skewed since large collections of field metrics have many outliers.
- **Focus on percentiles.** The 75th, 90th, and 95th percentiles are especially valuable, as these intervals tend to emphasize slower experiences over faster ones.
- **Pay special attention to the 90th percentile and up.** This is where you'll see how slower devices and poor network conditions affect performance. Address pain points in this range, and you'll make your website faster for everyone regardless of how fast their network connection or device is.

- **Contextualize the data.** Metrics alone only convey simplistic conclusions like, "This is when your page is interactive." If you're evaluating a vendor product, see if it collects device information and long-task data from the Long Tasks API. If you're rolling your own, store that data yourself. It will give you more insight into why some users experience trouble where others don't.

If you follow only one piece of advice, focus on percentiles! Percentiles are valuable in summarizing the range of outcomes in field metrics. Let's say we have a website with relatively little JavaScript with 312 LCP records:

PERCENTILE	LARGEST CONTENTFUL PAINT
25th	237 milliseconds
50th	619 milliseconds
75th	1,503 milliseconds
90th	3,693 milliseconds
95th	8,120 milliseconds

If we average all the records, we get about 1,707 milliseconds. While this is hardly a bad LCP score, it's a conglomeration of values that don't reflect an actual session. It lands near the 75th percentile, as the values in higher percentiles skew the average upward. Meanwhile, a whole 5 percent of outcomes from the 95th percentile and up reflect speeds that are at least six times slower than the 75th percentile!

Analyzing field metrics is tough, but it's rewarding when you see how different conditions describe your website's performance in ways synthetic tools can't. You can't use JavaScript responsibly without knowing how your website affects those who use it!

SHIFTING THE FOCUS

Assessing JavaScript performance is a vast subject that sprawls well beyond the scope of this chapter—hell, even this book! Still, the information here should be enough to get you up and running with more than the bare necessities. By now, you have an idea of key performance metrics, what it takes to assess both loading and runtime performance, and how JavaScript is involved in that whole soup of quantifying what is—and isn't—a good user experience.

Going forward, we'll focus on what it takes to relegate JavaScript to its appropriate role in your website for the benefit of your users. After all, those who depend on what you build don't necessarily care how you built something, only that it's fast and usable. Performance metrics and profiling explain what your performance picture looks like, but now we'll learn how to make it better.

4 BUILDING FOR SPEED

LIKE MANY OTHER SPECIES OF WASP, the paper wasp builds its nest by chewing up wood pulp and spitting it back out to use as a sort of unholy mortar. It's a weird thing to parse out in your head—chewing up whatever sources of wood you can find and then puking it back up to build your house—but that's evolution for you.

Weirder still is that paper wasps don't have a strong preference for the *type* of pulp—they'll use whatever's suitable. As Italian entomologist Mattia Menchetti found out, if the only pulp source around is colored construction paper, wasps will make it work (**FIG 4.1**).

As developers, we must also get creative with the tools and techniques available to us to keep our websites fast in the face of an ever-sprawling adoption of JavaScript. We have to deliver functionality only when necessary by importing scripts at the time of need, adapt to people's preferences for reduced data usage, use resource hints to get a head start on loading JavaScript assets, and layer on enhancements that can speed up our websites in the places where it matters most.

Let's roll!

FIG 4.1: A group of paper wasps constructing a multicolored nest out of construction paper. Photograph courtesy of Mattia Menchetti (http://bkaprt.com/rjs39/04-01).

RESPONSIBLE FEATURE DELIVERY

Some scripts must be loaded at startup, while others can be loaded sometime later. Knowing the difference is a challenging aspect of using JavaScript responsibly. The web platform can't do that work for us, but it does provide a tool to load JavaScript on demand: dynamic imports.

Static versus dynamic imports

Before we get into dynamic imports, we should probably talk about static imports. Chances are good that you've seen `import` statements used in JavaScript like so:

```
import PageContainer from "./PageContainer.js";
import { BlogPost } from "./Components.js";
```

The `import` statements shown above are *static imports*. Static imports incorporate external modules into the scope of the current script. The first and second lines in the preceding code demonstrate how named and default exports are imported, respectively.

This shows the corresponding types of exports in action:

```
const PageContainer = () => { /* Omitted code */ };
const BlogPost = () => { /* Omitted code */ };

// Default export
export default PageContainer;

// Named export
export BlogPost;
```

Whether you use named or default exports is immaterial to understanding the limitations of static imports:

- The module specifier—that is, the string that comes after the `from` keyword that specifies the module's location—can only be a plain string.
- Static imports can only ever be present at the top of a file.

These limitations restrict static imports to loading code immediately regardless of whether that code is executed at startup. A more flexible version of the `import` syntax, *dynamic import*, was developed to address this limitation (http://bkaprt.com/rjs39/04-02).

Dynamic imports are similar to static imports, except they can be placed anywhere in your code, and they rely on promises:

```
import("/js/module.js").then(module => {
  // Access the default export
  module.default();

  // Access a named export
  module.namedModule();
}).catch(error => {
  // Something went wrong!
  console.warn(error);
});
```

While this syntax is more verbose than a static import, its greater flexibility means we can load additional JavaScript after startup at a time of our choosing. This gives us greater control over how much code we load at startup, which can have significant performance benefits.

Code splitting

Dynamic imports make *code splitting* possible (http://bkaprt.com/rjs39/04-03). Code splitting is a performance optimization where we split any JavaScript that isn't necessary at startup from the application logic and instead load it on demand from separate script assets.

"Why should I give a damn about code splitting?" you might say. Allow me to elaborate: chances are good that you're shipping some unused JavaScript. The HTTP Archive disclosed in their 2020 almanac that roughly 37 percent of JavaScript shipped by the median experience goes unused (http://bkaprt.com/rjs39/04-04). That's a lot of kilobytes taxing devices and frittering away metered data plans for no good reason. And that's the *median* experience—your projects may be shipping more unused JavaScript than that!

So split we must, and split we will! However, the first step of code splitting is finding opportunities. User interactions are almost always potential code-splitting opportunities, which means we'll be looking for event listeners that fire due to an explicit interaction.

Code tucked away in `click` events, such as JavaScript-driven form validation, is one such opportunity for code splitting. Scripts that run in `click` events are a prime example of *deferred behavior*, as the JavaScript associated with them doesn't run during startup. As the HTTP Archive shows, we often load scripts for these behaviors regardless of whether they'll be used, even though they can be loaded on demand instead.

Another good example of a deferred interaction is the `<form>` element's `submit` event. This event is a perfect opportunity to defer loading JavaScript with a well-placed dynamic import:

```
const contactForm = document.
  getElementById("contact-form");
const inputs = contactForm.querySelectorAll("input,
  textarea");

inputs.forEach(input => {
  input.removeAttribute("required");
  input.removeAttribute("pattern");
});

contactForm.addEventListener("submit", event => {
  event.preventDefault();

  import("/js/contact-form-validation.js").
  then(module => {
    const [state, errors] = module.
  isFormValid(inputs);

    if (state) {
      contactForm.submit();

      return;
    }

    // TODO: Error processing code here
  });
});
```

BUILDING FOR SPEED **77**

After clicking submit, you'll have to wait for the dynamic import to grab the validation script (a possible drawback we'll address in more detail later). All the same, it's a good dynamic import example as well as a great example of progressive enhancement in action.

Because the server sends `<form>` markup with the `required` and `pattern` attributes, we need to strip them out before our custom validation logic can work. However, if the validation script fails to load or execute, the form will still have *some* validation capabilities provided by HTML itself. Not ideal, but that redundant functionality still saves us a trip to the server to validate all the inputs (something you should be doing anyway).

In the form's `submit` event callback, we call `event.preventDefault()` to prevent the form from submitting. After that, we dynamically import our validation module from the network, which contains a single named export called `isFormValid`. This export is a function, which in turn accepts the form's `<input>` elements, validates their contents, and returns an array containing the success state of the validation and any errors.

This is but one type of interaction where dynamic import is useful. If you have a lot of features on your website, there are likely more interaction points to consider, such as `click`, `hover`, `focus`, and `blur`.

Selectively polyfilling features

Polyfilling is the practice of using JavaScript to provide specific web-platform APIs in browsers that don't support them. It's often a necessary practice, but it also increases the amount of unused JavaScript if you're not careful to target delivery of those polyfills to only those browsers that require them.

Various parts of the Internationalization API are good examples of this. `Intl.relativeTimeFormat` is useful because it automatically generates relative time strings like "3 days ago" for English locales—or a whole slew of other ones:

```
const relativeTimeFormatter = new Intl.
  RelativeTimeFormat("de");
```

```
relativeTimeFormatter.format(-3, "day");   // "vor 3
  Tagen"
relativeTimeFormatter.format(3, "day");    // "in 3
  Tagen"
```

This functionality is a great fit for things like social media feeds. Because `Intl.relativeTimeFormat` provides this capability across a variety of locales, a common (yet complicated) task is handled by the browser's internals without the need for heavy libraries such as Moment.js, which weighs in at nearly 300 kilobytes (http://bkaprt.com/rjs39/04-05).

At the time of writing, not all browsers support Internationalization APIs. Polyfills exist for features like `Intl.relativeTimeFormat` and its dependencies within the broader API. However, depending on how much you need to polyfill, you might be sending twenty or more kilobytes of JavaScript that could go unused in some browsers, which can make startup slower—and that's to say nothing of the large scripts necessary for each locale, which is where the dragons lurk in this situation.

We can lean on dynamic import to keep unnecessary polyfilling from happening, which the maintainers of the Internationalization API polyfills already demonstrate how to do in Node.js development environments (http://bkaprt.com/rjs39/04-06):

```
import { shouldPolyfill } from "@formatjs/intl-
  relativetimeformat/should-polyfill"

async function polyfill (locale) {
  if (shouldPolyfill()) {
    await import("@formatjs/intl-relativetimeformat/
  polyfill")
  }

  if (Intl.RelativeTimeFormat.polyfilled) {
    switch (locale) {
      default:
        await import("@formatjs/intl-
  relativetimeformat/locale-data/en");
        break;
```

```
        case "fr":
          await import("@formatjs/intl-
    relativetimeformat/locale-data/fr");
          break;
      }
    }
  }
```

This code snippet handles polyfilling `Intl.relativeTime-Format` for a website where both English and French locales are used. Here, we import a utility method from the polyfill appropriately named `shouldPolyfill`. If this method determines that the polyfill is indeed necessary, it polyfills `Intl.relativeTimeFormat` and then dynamically imports locale data based on the value of `locale`.

This is far from the only case where dynamic import can be used to selectively polyfill web-platform features. Any time you reach for a polyfill, do a little research and check Can I Use (http://bkaprt.com/rjs39/04-07) to see how well supported the feature you're polyfilling is. Then, make an informed decision about how best to proceed.

Whether you use dynamic imports to conditionally polyfill browser APIs or defer your application scripts until they're needed, the result is the same: you're reducing the amount of JavaScript loaded during startup, which lessens processing and blocking time during that process.

GETTING A HEAD START

If your website relies heavily on JavaScript, the obstinate nature of networks means that the latency involved with requesting scripts will prolong the startup phase. To get ahead of this whole mess and alleviate the pain that comes with high-latency environments, we can employ one (or more) of a few techniques. In short, the sooner we can fetch those scripts, the faster the browser can process them.

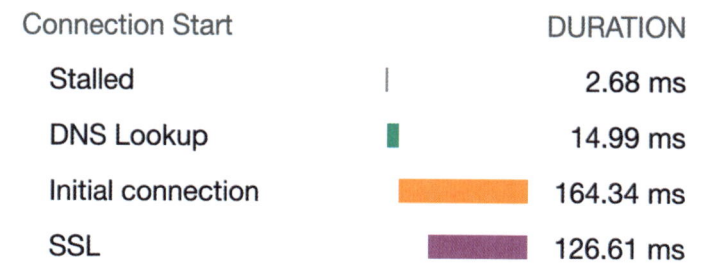

Connection Start		DURATION
Stalled	|	2.68 ms
DNS Lookup	▮	14.99 ms
Initial connection	▬▬▬	164.34 ms
SSL	▬▬	126.61 ms

FIG 4.2: The latency involved in various stages of connecting to a web server as shown in the network tab of Chrome's developer tools.

Self-hosting: One boringly effective trick

Loading performance is all about connections, and there's an elaborate dance that happens when browsers open connections to web servers (**FIG 4.2**):

1. A domain must be resolved to the web server's IP address through a DNS lookup.
2. Most web servers communicate over the *transmission control protocol* (TCP). TCP connections take time to establish, and both the TCP handshake and the slow start factor into how quickly a web server can respond (http://bkaprt.com/rjs39/04-08).
3. If HTTPS is involved, *transport layer security* (TLS) negotiation will also take time.

HTTP/3 reduces the latency involved in connection and TLS negotiation. While that's great, there will always be *some* latency, HTTP/3 or otherwise. That's why self-hosting is a boringly effective performance enhancement not just for JavaScript but for *all* asset types.

Self-hosting is worth discussing since it's not uncommon to see assets loaded from public CDNs like cdnjs (http://bkaprt.com/rjs39/04-09). Although public CDNs can be useful because they remove the burden of hosting popular libraries and frameworks, you must weigh the latency cost of adding another

BUILDING FOR SPEED   81

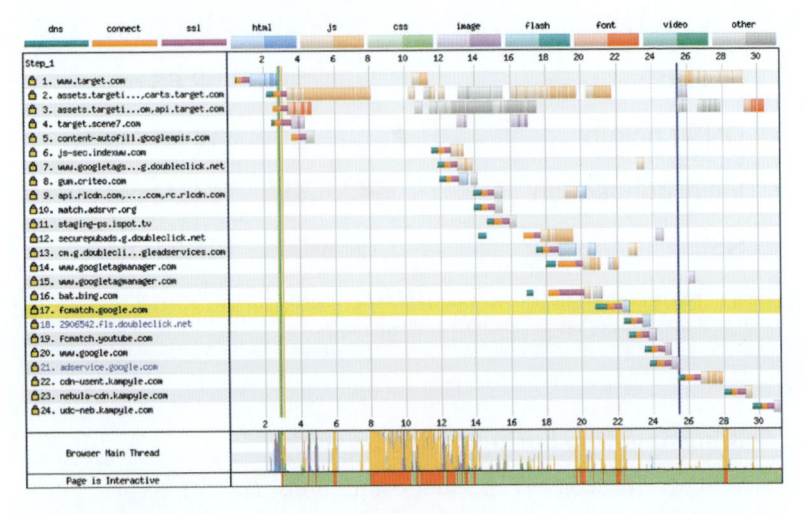

FIG 4.3: WebPageTest's connection view listing all origins used in a website. Each row represents a separate connection, displaying DNS lookup (teal), connection (orange), and TLS negotiation time (purple).

---

cross-origin—that is, any web server other than your own—against hosting your own assets (**FIG 4.3**).

A common misconception is that public CDNs provide an additional performance benefit due to *shared caching*. Shared caching is the idea that if you visit a website that requests, say, a copy of React hosted on a public CDN, that same copy of React should be pulled from the browser cache if another website requests it from the same location.

While that would be a welcome optimization in theory, it doesn't exist in practice because browsers key the primary origin—that is, your web server—against requests for cross-origin resources, resulting in a cache miss (http://bkaprt.com/rjs39/04-10). There's no upside for using public CDNs from a performance respective.

Where JavaScript is concerned, self-hosting shortens the loading phase by reducing latency, meaning the browser can get on with the processing phase sooner.

82 RESPONSIBLE JAVASCRIPT

Greasing the skids with resource hints

There are situations in which self-hosting may not always be practically possible, and that's where resource hints can help reduce latency for cross-origin assets. *Resource hints* use the HTML `<link>` element to guide the browser to fetch resources or open connections to cross-origins earlier. Their use is instrumental in speeding up JavaScript loading so that websites can become interactive faster.

Reduce connection latency

Source order describes the order of elements in your HTML, and its importance can be overlooked when it comes to JavaScript performance. As we've often been told, it's best to place your `<script>` elements just before the closing `</body>` tag to avoid blocking rendering. However, this affects how long it takes the browser to discover them.

Browsers stream HTML and chunk up that parsing work into manageable pieces. Because of this, references to scripts located at the end of the markup won't be discovered until the browser parses them. When those scripts live on cross-origins, this adds significant latency to cross-origin asset retrieval (**FIG 4.4**).

With `preconnect`, however, we can open cross-origin connections as soon as the server starts streaming HTML by putting resource hints in the document `<head>`:

```
<link rel="preconnect" href="https://syndication.
  twitter.com/" rel="preconnect">
<link rel="preconnect" href="https://pbs.twimg.com/"
  rel="preconnect">
<link rel="preconnect" href="https://www.google-
  analytics.com/" rel="preconnect">
```

This improves performance by negotiating connections to cross-origin assets sooner, rather than waiting for the browser to discover references to them in due course (**FIG 4.5**).

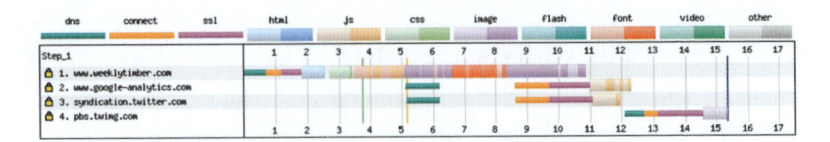

FIG 4.4: WebPageTest's connection view for a website. Rows two and three are for cross-origins where connections aren't established until the assets they provide are discovered by the HTML parser.

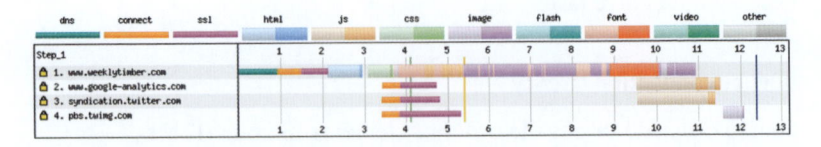

FIG 4.5: WebPageTest's connection view showing connection negotiation for cross-origin requests occurring earlier due to preconnect resource hints, resulting in roughly a three-second improvement in load time.

When self-hosting assets isn't possible, preconnect is an alternative that can take a bite out of the latency incurred by loading cross-origin assets. It's an effective and easy performance optimization that has more impact than you might think.

Preload critical JavaScript

The *critical path* is a concept in web performance that describes the number of requests needed to start rendering the core content of a page (http://bkaprt.com/rjs39/04-11). HTML and CSS files are typical examples of requests that are on the critical path, since you don't have much of a page without them (FIG 4.6).

CSS and HTML aren't the only asset types that can be on the critical path. In Chapter 2, we talked about how client-rendered markup is more expensive than markup provided by the server. Beyond the computational expense of parsing and executing JavaScript to render it, client-rendered markup is also a performance liability in that it puts JavaScript in the critical path. It's a regrettably common pattern (FIG 4.7).

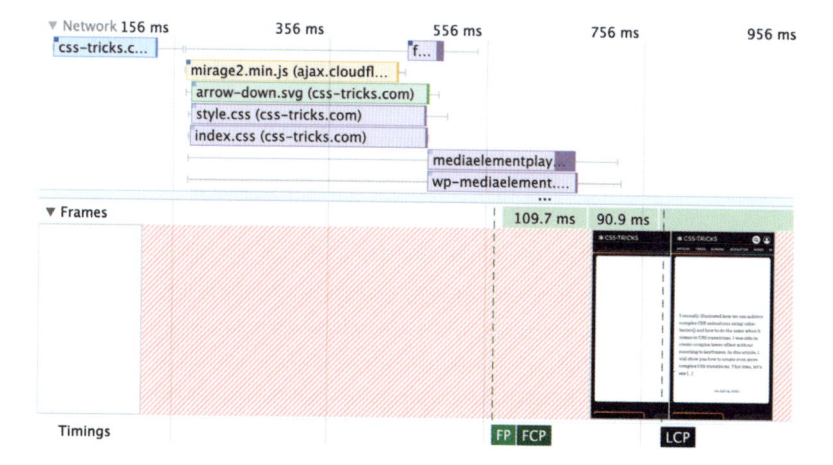

FIG 4.6: Critical requests for HTML and CSS (shown in the network pane at the top) shaded in blue and purple, respectively) for CSS-Tricks in Chrome's performance profiler. These assets are necessary before the page paints—shown in the timings pane at the bottom as FP and FCP.

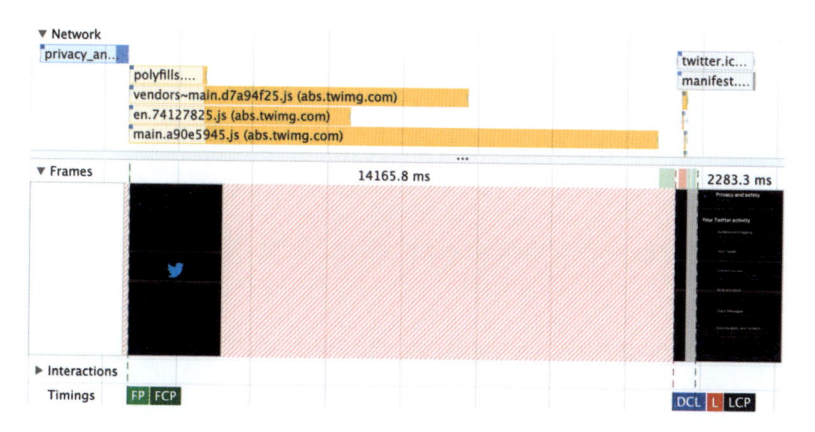

FIG 4.7: Critical JavaScript requests holding up the rendering of the mobile Twitter web app's settings page. While the loading screen appears quickly, the browser must wait for scripts to load—shown in the top pane in yellow—before the page fully renders.

BUILDING FOR SPEED   **85**

Fortunately, the `preload` resource hint helps to mitigate this issue by loading resources before the browser would normally discover them.

Say you have a page where you load two scripts before the closing `</body>` tag. The first contains vendor scripts—think frameworks and libraries. The second contains your application logic:

```
<script src="/js/vendors.ae6fd23c.js"></script>
<script src="/js/scripts.1db3ef48.js"></script>
```

`preload` gets around waiting for the HTML parser by changing the browser's discovery order of page assets:

```
<link rel="preload" as="script" href="/js/vendors.
  ae6fd23c.js">
<link rel="preload" as="script" href="/js/
  scripts.1db3ef48.js">
```

With these hints in the `<head>`, the browser will find these scripts sooner than if we otherwise waited for it to discover them near the end of the document. By the time the browser encounters the corresponding `<script>` elements at the bottom of the page, they'll be at least partially loaded.

Why, yes, there *are* caveats with `preload`:

- Read this, then *re*read it: if JavaScript is required to display critical content on your website, you're already in trouble. `preload` can be a salve for your JavaScript-induced loading performance woes, but other critical resources (i.e., stylesheets, webfonts, etc.) will be deprived of bandwidth because you have effectively reprioritized JavaScript over them. Get to the source of the problem—JavaScript, that is—and remove it from the critical path by having the server provide that contentful markup instead of relying on client rendering (http://bkaprt.com/rjs39/04-12).
- `preload` hints require an `as` attribute to describe the nature of the asset (http://bkaprt.com/rjs39/04-13). For scripts, this

value should be `script`. If you're an `as`hole and don't specify `as`, the preloaded response will be discarded.
- Because `preload`s are given higher priority, other requests could be deprived of bandwidth. Use `preload` sparingly. If everything is high priority, nothing is.
- If you're preloading a JavaScript module—that is, a script loaded by a `<script>` element with a `type` attribute value of `module`—you don't want `preload`. Instead, you want `modulepreload`, which follows the same format as `preload`, but without any of that `as` attribute business. There are also parsing benefits that come with `modulepreload` that you don't get with `preload`, such as recursively preloading an entire module tree, as well as speculative parsing benefits (http://bkaprt.com/rjs39/04-14).

Caveats aside, `preload` is effective, especially for critical JavaScript in web-app architectures, which—quite frankly—need all the help they can get to be performant. Use it responsibly, and as always, measure the benefits to see if it's right for your project.

Preload on-demand JavaScript

Remember earlier when we were yakkin' about code splitting and dynamic import? Well, one of the drawbacks of that whole scenario is that if you defer loading a script right up until the second it's needed, those on slow network connections will find themselves waiting for your dynamic import to complete before the action they've taken kicks off.

This doesn't mean code splitting is an antipattern; it just means we need to do a little thinking about how to solve the latency drawback. Consider the example of the contact form from earlier that relied on a dynamic import to retrieve the form validation script on submit. There's a bit of a delay before the form validation script downloads and runs (**FIG 4.8**).

This delay is frustrating: when someone submits the form, they expect a signal from the page that their interaction is being processed. Except there's no indication *anything* is happening until some script they don't know about has loaded.

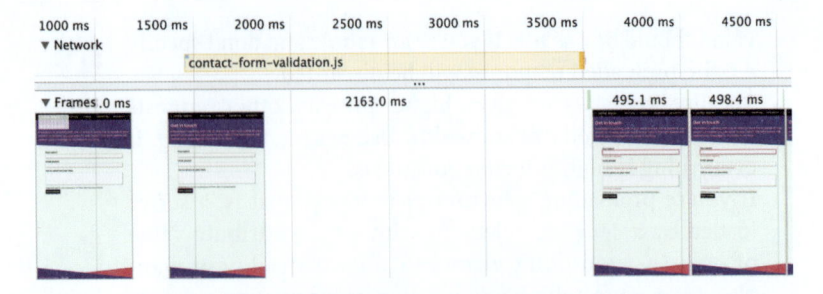

FIG 4.8: In this performance profiling session, it takes roughly two seconds to download the form validation script, delaying validation.

This hypothetical situation doesn't invalidate the performance benefit of a well-placed dynamic import, but we do need to adjust our strategy. Let's start with a small function that injects a `preload` into the document `<head>` on demand:

```
function injectPreload (href, module, as) {
  let preloadHint = document.createElement("link");
  preloadHint.rel = module ? "modulepreload" :
  "preload";
  preloadHint.href = href;

  if (!module && typeof as !== "undefined") {
    preloadHint.as = as;
  }

  document.head.appendChild(preloadHint);
}
```

This function takes three arguments:

1. The location of the script to preload
2. A Boolean for whether the script is a module; If so, the resource hint will be a `modulepreload` rather than a `preload`
3. The value to populate the hint's `as` attribute

88 RESPONSIBLE JAVASCRIPT

When run, this function constructs the resource hint and injects the generated `<link>` element into the `<head>`. This kicks off a request to get the script.

All that's left is to find the right moment to kick off the preload. Since this is a form, the opportune moment is whenever a form field is focused; the user action of filling out the form fields buys us some time:

```
const inputs = Array.from(document.
  querySelectorAll("#contact-form input, .contact-
  form textarea"));
let preloaded = false;

inputs.forEach(input => {
  input.addEventListener("focus", () => {
    if (!preloaded) {
      injectPreload("/js/contact-form-validation.
  js", false, "script");
      preloaded = true;
    }
  }, {
    once: true
  })
});
```

This ensures our form-validation script will only be preloaded when someone focuses any of the inputs in the form, but only once. This is an exercise in gauging intent: if someone has focused a form field, they probably intend to fill out the form, and the preload will likely finish before they do.

Once the form is submitted and the dynamic import kicks off, the validation script will already be in the browser cache. This means the dynamic import will hit the browser cache instead of the network, rendering the interaction practically instantaneous (**FIG 4.9**).

This opportunistic approach takes advantage of code splitting while also minimizing the delays involved when we defer the loading of scripts. This is as close as we'll get to having our cake *and* eating it.

BUILDING FOR SPEED **89**

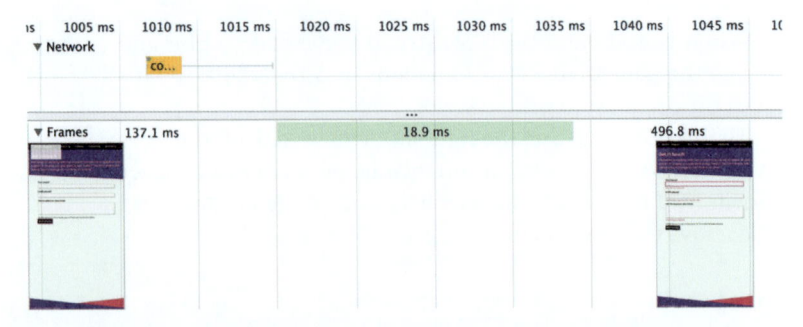

FIG 4.9: The latency involved in retrieving the form validation script with a dynamic import is practically eliminated due to preloading that script prior to the form's submission.

The goal with resource hints in general is this: if we do all that we can as developers to ease JavaScript's ill effects during startup, we can improve both loading and runtime performance. Remember, the word *responsible* is the load-bearing word in *Responsible JavaScript*. Resource hints are yet another tool in the box to help us live up to that obligation.

HELP PEOPLE SAVE DATA

Imagine how much easier our work would be if we developed for a single piece of hardware. Were that the case, this book wouldn't need to exist. We would have figured out how to use JavaScript responsibly by now.

But, aw *hell*, we develop for tons of devices and network conditions. Constraints vary from user to user, which makes building performant architectures incredibly challenging—but we owe it to our users to adapt to their needs.

If you've spent even a minute in the rural United States, you know that finding a fast and reliable network connection can be a nightmare (http://bkaprt.com/rjs39/04-15). In these internet voids, people may state a preference for reduced data usage to alleviate the pain of browsing on slow networks. This goes a long way toward making the web faster for those who have the deck stacked against them—if we can accommodate them.

Signals for reduced data usage

On the Android version of Google Chrome, users can specify a preference for reduced data usage via "Data Saver Mode" or "Lite Mode." When enabled, this mode does two things:

1. Chrome sets `navigator.connection.saveData` to `true`.
2. Chrome sends a `Save-Data` HTTP header with a value of `on` for every request.

Historically, that platform was the only one to offer such a mode, but more recently the `prefers-reduced-data` media query in CSS has emerged to expand data-saving functionality to all browsers. It can have a value of either `no-preference`, which communicates no preference for data usage, or `reduce`, which reduces data usage.

In Chrome for Android, the reduced-data-usage preference adheres to the standardized `prefers-reduced-data` media query. While it may seem like a CSS feature doesn't have much use in JavaScript, we can evaluate this preference through the `matchMedia` method:

```
// If a preference for reduced data usage is
  specified,
// this expression will evaluate to true:
const saveData = window.matchMedia("(prefers-
  reduced-data: reduce)").matches;
```

If you've gleaned anything from this book so far, though, it's that the role of JavaScript is one to be reduced, not expanded. Given that, it seems more reasonable to read the `Save-Data` request header on the server. It's not that this value has no relevance in JavaScript itself—indeed, it does! It's just that your best bet to reduce your reliance on JavaScript is on the server. In a backend language—such as PHP—the `Save-Data` header can be detected like so:

FIG 4.10: The full-featured version of Weekly Timber's Q&A page has a carousel and JavaScript-powered accordions.

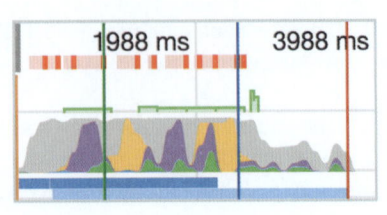

FIG 4.11: The main-thread activity overview in Chrome's performance profiler for the Weekly Timber website's Q&A page. The page kicks off a not-inconsequential amount of JavaScript activity as well as JavaScript-induced layout and paint work.

```
define("SAVE_DATA", isset($_SERVER["HTTP_SAVE_
    DATA"]) && stristr($_SERVER["HTTP_SAVE_DATA"],
    "on") !== false);
```

This snippet defines a SAVE_DATA constant. From there, this signal can be used on the backend to focus on the page's critical content and strip out nonessential assets—including JavaScript.

We can see this in action on the website for Weekly Timber, a Wisconsin logging company. The Q&A page features a carousel and accordions (**FIG 4.10**), which both depend on jQuery, and the carousel has a big chunk of JavaScript driving it. There's also the carousel plugin itself as well as a small bit of JavaScript to initialize it all.

92   RESPONSIBLE JAVASCRIPT

These enhancements total up to slightly fewer than 100 kilobytes of uncompressed JavaScript. It's not an egregious amount of JavaScript as far as web pages go, but it does spur quite a bit of main-thread activity on slow devices (**FIG 4.11**).

But we can use the SAVE_DATA constant we created to strip the bells and whistles for Weekly Timber's customers, who may be in less-than-ideal rural network conditions. We opted to remove the carousel and the accordion functionality if the SAVE_DATA constant is true, as well as the entirety of the carousel markup:

```php
<?php
if (!SAVE_DATA) {
  ?>
  <section id="carousel">
    <!-- Carousel markup omitted -->
  </section>
  <?php
}
?>
```

And hell, if the markup for the carousel isn't necessary—or if we're not going to use the accordion functionality for the Q&A content—we can exclude scripts if SAVE_DATA is true as well:

```php
if (!SAVE_DATA) {
  ?>
  <script src="/js/jquery.js"></script>
  <script src="/js/carousel.js"></script>
  <script src="/js/accordion.js"></script>
  <script src="/js/q-and-a.js"></script>
  <?php
}
```

If someone with a specified preference for reduced data usage happens by this page, they'll get an experience that spares none of the core content (**FIG 4.12**).

BUILDING FOR SPEED

FIG 4.12: The light version of the Weekly Timber FAQ page, served to those with a preference for reduced data usage, strips out the carousel and accordions.

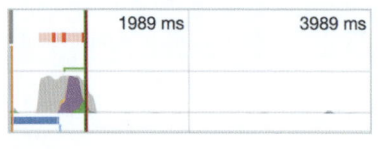

FIG 4.13: The main-thread activity overview in Chrome's performance profiler for the Weekly Timber Q&A page with data saving enabled.

Abiding by a preference for reduced data usage can also have a measurable effect on the main-thread work. In Weekly Timber's case, a visitor on a slower device with data saving enabled would enjoy a user experience with far less main-thread activity (**FIG 4.13**).

Hopefully it's clear that carousels and accordions aren't the only features you can omit in the presence of this preference. If you embrace progressive enhancement, you can apply this to almost *any* progressively enhanced interaction by omitting JavaScript. It's your call!

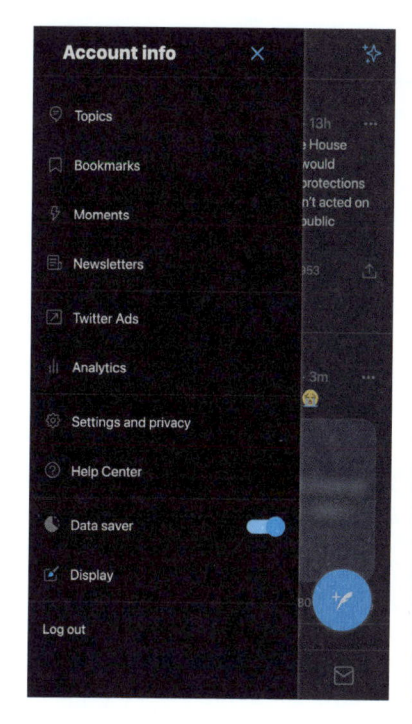

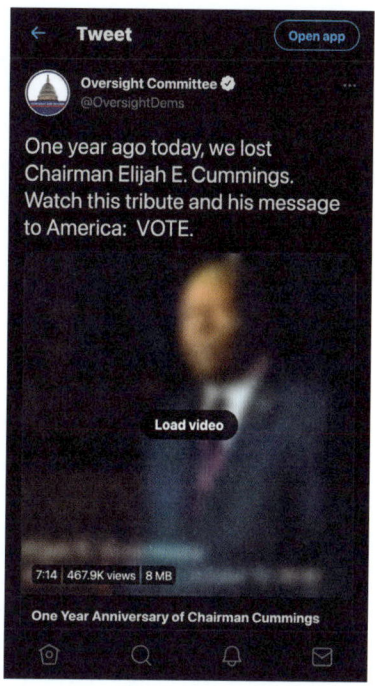

FIG 4.14: Twitter's Data saver setting is located near the bottom of its mobile navigation menu.

FIG 4.15: Twitter's data saver feature in action. Here, visitors can decide what media they wish to download to conserve data usage.

Saving data as a custom feature

Data-saving functionality doesn't have to be provided only by the browser; you can build it into your own application as a toggleable setting so that everyone can benefit from it, not just those on browsers that offer it. For example, Twitter offers an application-level setting to help visitors save data (**FIG 4.14**).

With this setting enabled, Twitter downloads ultra-low-resolution placeholders for images and videos, then allows users to choose whether they want to view the associated media (**FIG 4.15**).

BUILDING FOR SPEED   **95**

How you implement a custom-built data saver feature depends on your project. You can store it on a per-machine basis in a cookie or in JavaScript using `localStorage` (http://bkaprt.com/rjs39/04-16). Or, if you want to broaden access to this feature as much as possible, you can store this preference in an application's backend.

The conceptual simplicity of a data saver is what gives it power: if you offer people a chance to opt into reduced data usage, there's a good chance they'll take you up on it. It's an opportunity to give people more control over their experience *and* reduce your use of JavaScript on their behalf.

RESILIENCY: THY NAME IS SERVICE WORKER

If you've ever installed ceramic tile, you know that it's a hell of a process. First, you ensure your subfloor is level. Then you lay down a decoupling membrane on the subfloor. Then you put down a mortar bed. Then you back-butter tiles and set them in the mortar bed. Then you grout. Then you seal the grout. It's a lot of work, but that work adds strength, resiliency, and appeal to the finished installation.

The process of building resilient websites as we've described it so far in this book is similarly redundant and layered. Yet, there's one more layer we should consider adding: a service worker (http://bkaprt.com/rjs39/04-17).

Service Worker is an API that acts as a proxy between the browser and the server. Service workers are powerful little cogs that can intercept requests and responses, reroute requests, cache responses, and provide offline capability to make a website not only more accessible in more places but also faster.

Prioritizing speed and access

Weekly Timber is situated in Waushara County, Wisconsin. Good network connections can be hard to come by out in a place like this (**FIG 4.16**).

There's farmland in Wisconsin, yes, but there's also tons of forest. If you need some trees cut down, you'll hit up Google

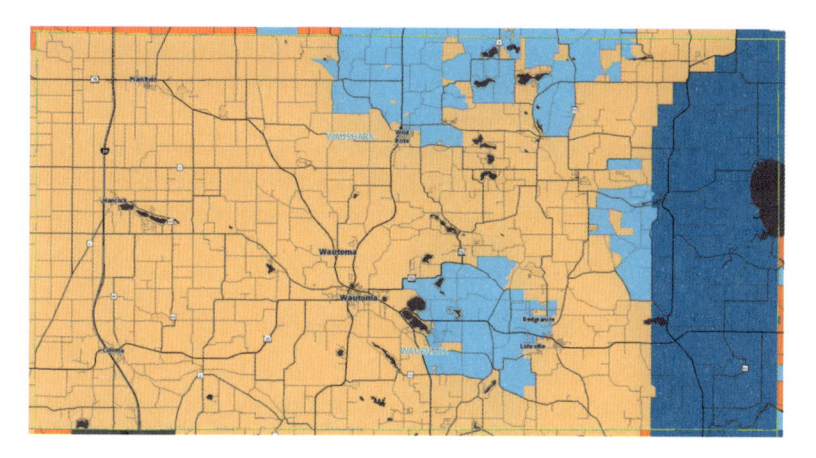

FIG 4.16: A broadband color overlay map of Waushara County, Wisconsin. Most of the county is shown in tan, which indicates broadband speeds between 3 and 9.99 Mbps. Areas in light blue and dark blue are faster.

and look for a logging company. How fast a logging company's website loads—or doesn't—may factor into whether you give that company a call.

This is where a service worker tuned for speed and resiliency helps. I built a service worker for Weekly Timber that significantly improved perceptual performance by:

- precaching header and footer markup during the service worker's installation;
- requesting only content markup and assembling it with the precached header and footer markup;
- streaming the fully assembled response to get markup to the browser as fast as possible; and
- avoiding service worker startup delays by using navigation preload (http://bkaprt.com/rjs39/04-18).

The performance impact of these architectural decisions was pronounced. When this service worker was deployed for Weekly Timber, it resulted in 42 percent and 48 percent decreases in the median time to First Contentful Paint and Largest Contentful Paint, respectively. Better yet, these improve-

BUILDING FOR SPEED   97

ments were observed not by a synthetic performance testing tool but by people who actually use Weekly Timber's website (http://bkaprt.com/rjs39/04-19).

Before we can get into how we built this service worker, though, we'll need to establish a cache for it—because without a cache, a service worker won't do you a whole lot of good from a performance standpoint.

Establishing a service worker cache

Service workers rely on the `Cache` interface (http://bkaprt.com/rjs39/04-20), which provides a caching layer distinct from the browser cache we covered in Chapter 3. When a service worker installs, its `install` event fires (http://bkaprt.com/rjs39/04-21). This is where we create a new service worker cache:

```
self.addEventListener("install", event => {
  const cacheName = "fancy_cache_name_here";
  const cachedAssets = [
    "/partial-header",
    "/partial-footer"
  ];

  event.waitUntil(caches.open(cacheName).then(cache => {
    return cache.addAll(cachedAssets);
  }));
});
```

There are two things going on here:

1. Our service worker cache needs a unique identifier, which we specify in `cacheName`. We use this identifier to open a cache with the `Cache` interface's `open` method (http://bkaprt.com/rjs39/04-22) so we can track what we put in it.
2. After we open a new cache, we can precache assets in it using the `Cache` interface's `addAll` method (http://bkaprt.com/rjs39/04-23). We can populate it with anything we think is worth loading ahead of time. In this minimal example,

we precache the markup for the header and footer of the Weekly Timber website.

Ideally, you'd autogenerate your service worker's cache identifier at build time so you don't have to manually change it on every update. For Weekly Timber's service worker, I used a text replacement plugin in my toolchain to inject the current value of +Date.now() as the cache name (http://bkaprt.com/rjs39/04-24).

Things can get hairy if you also want to precache versioned assets. We talked about these assets in Chapter 3, where file names are hash-based and look something like home.3afd5e1c.css. To get around this, you can use a bundler—a tool we'll cover in Chapter 5—to generate what's called an *asset manifest*, which is a JSON object of file names, and import this into your service worker.

Activating the service worker

In the service worker life cycle, activation comes after installation. Activation is an opportunity to do some housekeeping, which happens in a service worker's activate event:

```
self.addEventListener("activate", event => {
  const cacheName = "fancy_cache_name_here";
  const preloadAvailable = "navigationPreload" in
  self.registration;

  event.waitUntil(caches.keys().then(keys => {
    return Promise.all([
      keys.filter(key => {
        return key !== cacheName;
      }).map(key => {
        return caches.delete(key);
      }),
      preloadAvailable ? self.registration.
  navigationPreload.enable() : true
    ]);
  }));
});
```

There are some asynchronous processes that will eventually resolve within the `activate` event, so we pass an array of them to `Promise.all`:

1. The `activate` event is where we do some housekeeping. Because a service worker can be updated with a new cache identifier later, we'll want to take this opportunity to retrieve an array of the currently registered caches using the `Cache` interface's `keys` method (http://bkaprt.com/rjs39/04-25). With this array, we can prune old caches with expired identifiers with the `Cache` interface's `delete` method (http://bkaprt.com/rjs39/04-26).
2. Service worker bootup time can delay requests. `navigationPreload` gets around this by making service worker bootup and navigation requests concurrent rather than consecutive. Since it's not supported in all browsers, though, we store its support status in `preloadAvailable`, and use a ternary operator to explicitly enable `navigationPreload` where it's supported and pass a Boolean value where it isn't.

This is a whole lot of *stuff*, but we're just getting to the fun part: intercepting and modifying responses!

Intercepting requests

Intercepting network requests is the main event in a service worker. When combined with the `Cache` interface, the ability to intercept requests and customize responses is fertile ground for a fast user experience.

Before we get into handling specific request types, we need to start with a good default:

```
self.addEventListener("fetch", async event => {
  const { request } = event;

  if (request.method !== "GET") {
    return;
  }
```

```
    // Code omitted for brevity...
  });
```

`fetch` is another service worker event, and it fires whenever the browser dispatches a network request. In most cases, a good default is to check whether the `event` object's `request.method` property represents a `GET` request. `POST` requests are driven by user-specific actions, such as submitting forms. We don't want to operate on those requests, so we just pass them through the `fetch` event handler by throwing a `return`.

From here, we need to bifurcate our logic according to the type of content we're requesting: static assets or navigation.

Handling static assets

A "cache first, network second" pattern is a good default for handling static asset requests—that is, requests for assets that don't change in any context, like CSS, images, fonts, and, yeah, JavaScript.

This means that we'll first check to see if a static asset is in the service worker cache. The first request for it will fail, though, since the asset won't be in there yet; we'll have to hit the network to get it. After we do, we'll place the asset in the cache so future requests for it can bypass the network entirely.

This means that static asset retrieval from `Cache` interface is extremely fast (**FIG 4.17**). The logic for it is also reasonably simple and direct. You either have the asset in the cache or you don't. If you don't, you grab it and put it in the cache:

```
self.addEventListener("fetch", async event => {
  // Request filtering code omitted...

  const staticAssets =
  /\.(woff2?|css|m?js|gif|avif|webp|png|svg|jpe?g|txt|ico)$/i;

  if (staticAssets.test(request.url)) {
    event.respondWith(caches.match(request.url).
    then(cachedResponse => {
```

```
    return cachedResponse || fetch(request).
then(fetchedResponse => {
      addResponseToCache(request, fetchedResponse.
clone());

      return fetchedResponse;
    });
  }));

  return;
}

// More to come...
});
```

Just as `fetch` can be used in a main-thread context to retrieve assets, it can also be used in a service worker. This is exactly what we use to grab a static asset from the network if a cache seek fails with the `Cache` interface's `match` method (http://bkaprt.com/rjs39/04-27). If that fails, we use a small custom function called `addResponseToCache` to add the asset to the cache:

```
function addResponseToCache (request, response) {
  caches.open(CACHE_NAME).then(cache => {
    cache.put(request, response);
  });
};
```

Static asset handling is the simplest of all this request interception business. It's about to get a whole lot hairier as we figure out how we want to handle navigation requests.

Handling navigation requests

A navigation request is for an HTML document—that is, a request for an entirely different page, as opposed to a request for, say, an image or for some JavaScript. For Weekly Timber's service worker, we want to handle navigation requests much differently than static asset requests.

Service Worker		DURATION
Startup		0.16 ms
▶ respondWith		1.21 ms
Request/Response		DURATION
Waiting (TTFB)		1.55 ms
Content Download		2.21 ms
		4.14 ms

FIG 4.17: Request timings for a static asset stored in a service worker cache. Because the service worker doesn't have to go to the network to get the asset, it's served very quickly.

You'll recall earlier that we had a whole laundry list of requirements for Weekly Timber's service worker. Chief among them was that we wanted to reduce markup payloads. We do this by precaching header and footer markup—something we already did in the service worker's `install` event—and then combining them with content-only markup we request from the network (**FIG 4.18**).

This takes work, but it's possible—and honestly? The perceptual performance benefit you get in terms of both First Contentful Paint and Largest Contentful Paint justifies the effort—which, for Weekly Timber, ended up being 79 percent and 41 percent faster, respectively, than no service worker at all.

Let's get into how this request handling looks in our `fetch` event:

```
self.addEventListener("fetch", async event => {
  // Prior code omitted...

  if (request.mode === "navigate") {
    const networkContent = Promise.resolve(event.preloadResponse).then(response => {
      if (response) {
        addResponseToCache(request, response.clone());
```

```
      return response;
    }

    const headers = new Headers();
    headers.append("X-Content-Mode", "partial");

    return fetch(request.url, {
      headers
    }).then(response => {
      addResponseToCache(request, response.clone());

      return response;
    });
  }).catch(() => {
    return caches.match(request.url);
  });

  // More to come...
  }
});
```

There's a ton going on here. Let's break it down bit by bit:

1. To differentiate a navigation request from other requests, we can check the `request` object's `mode` property. If its value is `"navigate"`, we're on the right track.
2. If `navigationPreload` is supported, we can get its preloaded response in `event.preloadResponse`. If so, that's great! We can just add that response to the cache in case we're in an offline situation later. Navigation preload requests automatically send a `Service-Worker-Navigation-Preload` request with responses that we can use to have the backend send partial content.
3. The thing is, not all browsers support `navigationPreload`. If that's the case, `event.preloadResponse` is useless, and we'll have to adapt and make the request for the partial content markup ourselves. We'll also have to craft a custom `X-Content-Mode` header to instruct the backend to send partial

FIG 4.18: A color-coded representation of the header, content, and footer areas of the Weekly Timber website. The header (blue) and footer (red) areas of the site are served from the `Cache` interface and assembled into a single response with the content (yellow) area, which is requested from the network.

content, since the `Service-Worker-Navigation-Preload` header won't be sent in the absence of navigation preload.
4. If the request should fail for any reason (i.e., some offline tomfoolery) we'll serve up a page from the `Cache` interface. If it's there, that is.

We're almost there, but we've got one last thing to do: assemble that content markup with the header and footer markup we precached earlier. Then we can serve that as the complete response:

```javascript
self.addEventListener("fetch", event => {
  // Prior code omitted...

  if (request.mode === "navigate") {
    // Navigation preload/fetch() fallback code
    omitted...

    const { done, response } = await
    mergeResponses([
       caches.match("/partial-header"),
       networkContent,
       caches.match("/partial-footer")
    ]);

    event.waitUntil(done);
    event.respondWith(response);
  }
});
```

This the last little bit of our service worker `fetch` event code. While it's succinct, it's no less impactful:

1. `mergeResponses` is a custom function that takes an array of responses and merges them into one. The first and third array items are precached header and footer markup retrieved by the `Cache` interface's `match` method. The second item is the content markup from the network.
2. The internals of `mergeResponses` are too much of a monster to step through here, but the source is on GitHub (http://bkaprt.com/rjs39/04-28). In short, `mergeResponses` takes an array of responses and uses the ReadableStream API to begin streaming that content to the browser as soon as possible (http://bkaprt.com/rjs39/04-29). When finished, it returns an object with two properties: a promise that resolves when the responses have been assembled (`done`), and the assembled response that we send to the browser (`response`).

But all our work on this service worker won't do much good until we install it, which is the last part of this whole show.

Installing the service worker

While installing a service worker is the easiest part of this whole hootenanny, we do need to be cognizant of a couple things:

- Service worker support—while fantastic (http://bkaprt.com/rjs39/04-30)—isn't guaranteed. Do a little feature-checking to avoid errors on legacy browsers.
- Because a service worker may precache stuff for other pages, we want to make sure it isn't registered until the page loads.

These aren't horribly difficult issues to get around. Assuming our service worker is named `sw.js` and resides at the root, we can add this little bit of script at the bottom of every page:

```
<script>
  window.addEventListener("load", () => {
    if ("serviceWorker" in navigator) {
      navigator.serviceWorker.register("/sw.js");
    }
  });
</script>
```

By waiting until the `window`'s `load` event, we're reducing the chance that the service worker and whatever it precaches will contend for bandwidth with critical resources. By checking for the `serviceWorker` namespace in the `navigator` object, we're ensuring that we don't run any code that will cause problems on legacy browsers.

We're in deep with this whole service worker thing, but we've finally come to rest. Yes, it's a ton to take in and apply, and this is just one service worker example for one website. Even so, that service worker gave Weekly Timber some incredible perceptual performance benefits:

	NO SERVICE WORKER	STREAMING SERVICE WORKER	SPEED INCREASE
Median FCP (ms)	767	159	79.3%
Median LCP (ms)	853	466	54.6%
p95 FCP (ms)	3027	1497	45.4%
p95 LCP (ms)	3357	1764	47.5%

Better yet, service workers are a perfect example of progressive enhancement. They don't replace the browser's built-in navigation behavior, but improve upon it in a way that's customizable and additive. That's the very essence of what it means to use JavaScript responsibly.

FAST, RESILIENT, AND USER FIRST

It takes a lot nowadays to build engaging user experiences with a restrained use of JavaScript, but it's possible. Some of that effort involves sleight of hand, where we rely on less obvious approaches like resource hints to mask latency and loading time of page assets.

Other efforts involve more direct action, like reducing startup time through code splitting, or respecting user preferences for reduced data usage. In some cases, we may need to go above and beyond with a service worker that not only reduces data usage and offers offline access, but also improves page performance.

Nearly any architecture can benefit from the techniques we've covered. As you work with various tools, you'll likely run into toolchains that use your project's JavaScript to output production-ready assets. It behooves you to know how to navigate these toolchains, as they can affect your website's performance—for better or for worse. We'll touch on these shortly.

5 NAVIGATING TOOLCHAINS

CICADA KILLER WASPS ELICIT an almost pants-shitting level of fear for the uninitiated. They are monstrously large (**FIG 5.1**). They have to be, because—as their name suggests—they kill cicadas. Big prey takes a big predator.

But they're still smaller than the cicadas they hunt, which means that once they've caught and paralyzed their victim, they're physically unable to take off from the ground! If they aren't lucky enough to grab a cicada in midair, they must drag their prey to the top of a tree and jump. This is the only way for these wasps to get sufficient altitude to stabilize themselves for flying. It's a ton of effort, but for a big payoff.

Toolchains—that is, collections of utilities that transform and optimize our JavaScript for production use—can involve similarly herculean effort, both to use them effectively and to understand their potential effects on performance. While you don't *need* any of the tools mentioned in this chapter to build fast and delightful user experiences, you're likely to encounter them in your work. If we're to invest in using toolchains, we need to make it worth our while.

FIG 5.1: A cicada killer wasp with a paralyzed cicada. Photograph by Judy Gallagher (http://bkaprt.com/rjs39/05-01), CC BY 2.0 (http://bkaprt.com/rjs39/05-02), via Wikimedia Commons.

TASK RUNNERS

Let's ease into this thing by starting with *task runners*. Task runners are linear JavaScript build tools that don't analyze code. They're typically used to minify, concatenate, and otherwise optimize a directory of scripts (or other files) into production-ready assets (**FIG 5.2**).

Task runners are attractive because they're straightforward: you have a thing you want to do to some files, so you point the task runner at the files to do the thing. This linearity results in a low learning curve and quick adoption. For example, the A11Y Project relies on a popular task runner called gulp.js (http://bkaprt.com/rjs39/05-03), and they even promote it in their technology statement, citing "ease of set up [sic]" and "approachability for beginners" (http://bkaprt.com/rjs39/05-04).

110 RESPONSIBLE JAVASCRIPT

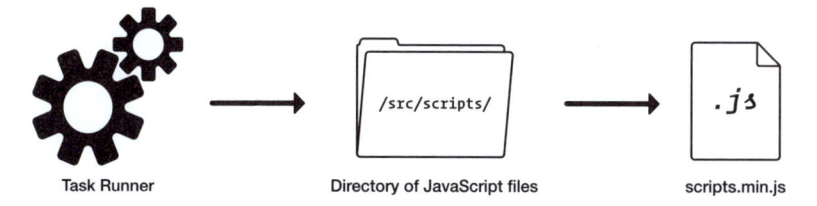

FIG 5.2: A typical task runner workflow. Here, the task runner is pointed at a directory of JavaScript files. The task runner minifies and concatenates all scripts in the directory into one production-ready script.

Task runners can be used anywhere, and they're an especially great fit for websites that don't rely heavily on JavaScript. But they aren't for every project. Since they apply broad optimizations to JavaScript files without analyzing their contents, they can't optimize your code in the more sophisticated ways that other tools can. That's where bundlers come in.

BUNDLERS

Using a task runner for a website that depends on JavaScript to function can lead to a lot of duplicated or unused code being served across different pages. If your project relies heavily on JavaScript, a bundler may be a better fit.

The primary tradeoff between task runners and bundlers is ease of use. Where task runners are easier to learn and set up, bundlers can get downright byzantine. I have personally observed webpack (http://bkaprt.com/rjs39/05-05) configurations of more than one hundred lines—sometimes many more. Other bundlers, such as Rollup (http://bkaprt.com/rjs39/05-06) or Parcel (http://bkaprt.com/rjs39/05-07), may be more straightforward than webpack but may not fit as well in certain architectures due to differing requirements.

No matter what bundler you choose, though, a key difference between these and task runners lies in how you'll want to structure your application logic.

How bundlers work

Instead of applying broad optimizations to a bunch of files, bundlers go through a project codebase and analyze its various static and dynamic `import`s. This means that a bundler sees your application as a collection of modules, unlike a task runner, which doesn't analyze your codebase.

Bundlers come to understand the structure of your codebase through a comprehensive process (**FIG 5.3**):

- Bundlers accept one or more *entry points* in their configuration. Think of an entry point as the trunk of a tree. Each branch represents an `import`—a concept we touched on in Chapter 4—where modules become part of your application.
- By analyzing an entry point and the various modules and scripts it imports, the bundler builds a *dependency graph*. Think of a dependency graph as the representation of your entry point's tree.
- Using the dependency graph, the bundler then emits optimal production-ready script assets. This may include automatically splitting your code into separate bundles or dropping unused code.

The complicated business of tree shaking

Muck around with bundlers long enough, and you'll eventually hear about *tree shaking*. Tree shaking is an optimization where a bundler analyzes your application and drops unused modules. The result—at least, the *intended* result—is that you ship less JavaScript to browsers.

Success isn't guaranteed, but if you know that unused parts of a codebase are still being bundled in your production build, you've got some options.

ESM all the way

Tree shaking only occurs if the module type you're using can be *statically analyzed*. Static analysis occurs when source code

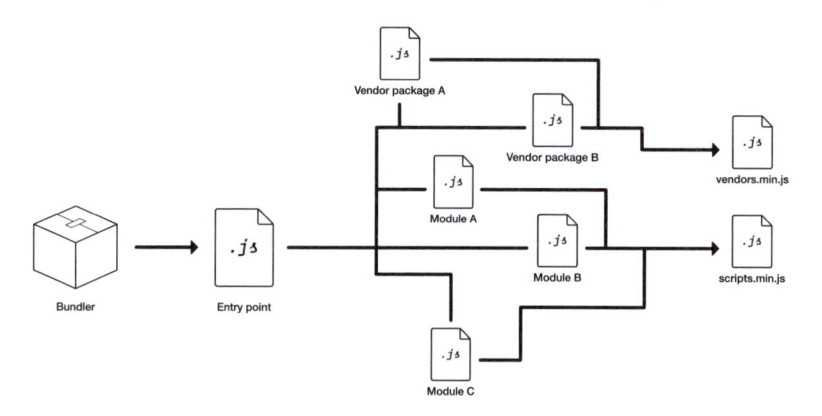

FIG 5.3: A bundler takes one or more entry points and builds a dependency graph, which it uses to decide how best to bundle scripts. Here, application modules and vendor modules—that is, scripts installed by npm—are bundled separately.

---

is analyzed by a compiler—the bundler, in this case—and a dependency tree can be built.

The types of modules you use play a pivotal role in how bundlers optimize output. Two common module types you'll encounter are *ES modules (ESM)* and *CommonJS modules*.

ESM may contain named and `default` exports, which can then be brought into another scope with the `import` statement:

```
// /js/build-script-tags.js
const buildScriptTags = scriptUrls => scriptUrls.
  map(url => '<script src="${url}"></script>');

export default buildScriptTags;

// /app.js
import buildScriptTags from "./js/build-script-tags.
  js";
```

CommonJS modules are similar, but rather than using the `export` statement, they use `module.exports`, and are imported using the `require` statement:

NAVIGATING TOOLCHAINS   **113**

```
// /js/build-script-tags.js
module.exports = scriptUrls => scriptUrls.map(url =>
  '<script src="${url}"></script>');

// /app.js
const buildScriptTags = require("./js/build-script-
  tags.js");
```

These differences may seem superficial. They're not. For one, ESM is supported in browsers *and* in later versions of Node.js, while CommonJS is only supported in Node.js. Second—and this is the kicker—CommonJS modules can't be statically analyzed. This is because both CommonJS's `module.exports` and `require` constructs accept dynamic expressions. Therefore, bundlers can't easily or reliably mark which CommonJS modules are unused (http://bkaprt.com/rjs39/05-08).

ESM resolves this via the static `import` statement, which can only accept a plain string. This makes tree shaking loads more predictable for bundlers.

Sometimes ESM becomes CommonJS

One reason tree shaking can fail is that a *transpiler*—that is, a tool that transforms modern JavaScript features and syntax into a legacy syntax that runs reliably in all browsers—may transform ESM modules to CommonJS for compatibility. How and when this happens depends on your configuration.

Babel is a transpiler that uses plugins and presets to transform JavaScript syntax. In Babel's ecosystem, a preset is a collection of plugins that achieve a certain output style. `preset-env` is a popular preset that transforms code according to the targeted environment (http://bkaprt.com/rjs39/05-09).

Depending on your configuration and aspects of your codebase, preset-env may inadvertently transform ESM to CommonJS. If this happens, your transpiled source ends up in a format that sidesteps static analysis, and tree shaking fails. As time goes on, this will be less likely, but just in case, we can instruct Babel to preserve module types with preset-env's `modules` setting:

```js
// babel.config.js
module.exports = {
  presets: [
    [
      "@babel/preset-env", {
        // Preserves module syntax:
        modules: false
      }
    ]
  ];
};
```

The potential downside of this is that it may create incompatible code with browsers that don't support ESM. For those browsers, you'll just have to take the hit if you can't justify dropping support for them, but, thankfully, those browsers are dropping in usage.

It's also worth assessing whether you need a transpiler in the first place. Depending on the project and its dependencies, you may be able to drop the transpiler from your toolchain altogether. As browsers mature and their support of new language features grows, this could be an increasingly viable option—*if* you can swing it.

Sometimes it's vendor code

Some vendor packages—often older ones—are written in CommonJS instead of ESM. This could be the package owner's stylistic preference, or a desire to maintain compatibility with more versions of Node.js. Whatever the reason, the outcome is that you're shipping more unused code. Your options here vary:

- If the package has suitable alternatives written in ESM, consider switching to one of those.
- If the package is a collection of utility functions and the license allows for it, you might be able to strip out the necessary parts of that library, convert them to ESM (if need be), and place that code directly into your project. Doing this reduces build size and production dependencies, and

also has the developer experience benefit of decreased install and build times.
- Can you write the functionality yourself? Some libraries offer methods that are now replaceable by built-in JavaScript methods. Chris Ferdinandi curates a collection of articles that show you how to accomplish many common tasks with nothing but bare JavaScript (http://bkaprt.com/rjs39/05-10).

Vendor packages may represent a significant portion of the JavaScript you ship to browsers. Whenever you encounter a vendor package that can't be optimized through tree shaking, it's a good idea to take a step back and consider your options.

When to externalize dependencies

You might see a lot of `import`s in a project. Each one signals the inclusion of one of two dependency types:

1. *Local dependencies* are code authored by you or your team and specific to your project. These are often not published as public dependencies anyone can install with a package manager.
2. *Remote dependencies* are code written outside of and often apart from your project. These are usually installed vendor packages, but your project architecture may isolate app-specific logic to installable—and possibly private—packages, an architectural style sometimes referred to as *micro frontends*.

Page speed suffers in micro-frontend architectures when vendor packages are duplicated across dependencies, which require extra effort to be eliminated, as the bundler's scope is restricted to each individual dependency.

Say your website uses React, but each component in your app is a remote dependency isolated in its own repository with its own toolchain. This causes each component to ship its own copy of React. That's a lot of redundant code.

To avoid duplicating code, you should *externalize* dependencies you know are provided from another source. All bundlers provide this functionality. For instance, webpack can externalize dependencies (http://bkaprt.com/rjs39/05-11) via its `externals` configuration:

```
module.exports = {
  // ...
  externals: {
    react: "React",
    "react-dom": "ReactDOM"
  }
};
```

Each key in the `externals` object is the name of an npm package, whose corresponding value is the namespace the package occupies in the global scope. With this in place, webpack won't bundle `react` and `react-dom`. It will instead skip them and assume you're providing those dependencies from another source at runtime.

While vendor code is a typical target for externalization, remote dependencies specific to your website are just as suitable. For example, consider an ecommerce retailer that uses a utility library in multiple components on its product detail page: if that utility library is not externalized in each dependency where it's used, its code will be duplicated throughout the site.

Some of this advice may give you the impression that bundlers are performance liabilities. While it's true that some bundlers tend to prioritize compatibility and interoperability in ways that can affect performance, that's no excuse to avoid them when it makes sense to use them. It just means you need to stay vigilant.

TRANSPILERS

We've already mentioned transpilers in this chapter, but they're a relevant tool you're likely to encounter in most toolchains. To recap, a transpiler transforms modern JavaScript features and syntax into a universally compatible syntax that runs reliably everywhere.

Transpilers, while understandably useful, can be just as thorny as bundlers if we use them carelessly. Whenever you transform a language feature to make it more compatible in more places, the transformed code will almost always have a larger footprint than its untransformed equivalent.

The business of transforms

Transpilers serve a special purpose in modern web development, as the addition of new features to JavaScript is at odds with the varying adoption of those features in browsers. Because of this, your project may use JavaScript features available in some browsers, but not others. These could be entirely new language constructs like classes or async/await, or even new operators like spread syntax.

Arrow functions and template literals are good examples of modern language features that may be transformed by a transpiler. Arrow functions provide a compact function syntax that's especially useful for callbacks, and template literals can conveniently incorporate JavaScript expressions into strings without concatenating operators:

```
const scriptTags = scriptUrls.map(url => '<script
  src="${url}"><\/script>').join("");
```

However, if a transpiler transforms the above code into a universally compatible syntax, the result is a more verbose, but practically equivalent, piece of code:

```
var scriptTags = scriptUrls.map(function (url) {
  return "<script src=\"".concat(url, "\"></
  script>");
}).join("");
```

While transpilers are helpful tools for ensuring cross-browser compatibility, they have a couple downsides:

- If a transpiler isn't configured to target your users' browsers, modern browsers may incur significantly more JavaScript overhead.
- Adding a transpiler to your toolchain—as well as understanding its potential performance impact—introduces a significant learning curve.

Transpilers are indispensable in cases where cross-platform compatibility is paramount, but they're not mandatory—though neither are any build tools, for that matter. If you're able to make architectural choices for a project, the pragmatic bet is always for incremental adoption.

Yet, the industry—and indeed, reality itself—is an unyielding bastard. You'll eventually have to deal with these tools at some point, if you haven't by now. Knowing how to rein them in can make a difference when it comes to JavaScript performance.

Transforms aren't free

Depending on its configuration, a transpiler can add bloat to your bundles when transforming any number of features: ES6 classes, async functions, spread syntax, default parameters, generator functions, and so forth, so long as JavaScript itself continues to evolve.

Let's kick the tires on this concept and start with default parameters. If you've been programming in any language long enough, you've probably observed that—depending on the language—a function's parameters can have defaults that'll kick in if they're omitted. Compared to other languages, this is a relatively new JavaScript feature:

```
function generateLinkTags (cssFiles = ["/css/global.
  css"]) {
  return cssFiles.map(cssFile => {
    return '<link rel="stylesheet"
  href="${cssFile}">';
  }).join("");
}
```

This function generates a string of `<link>` elements to include CSS files. On the first line, you'll see that the `cssFiles` parameter is followed by an equal sign and an array containing a reference to a global CSS file. This means that the function can be run without any arguments and a default will kick in. This is a useful feature in many situations.

When this function is processed by Babel, though, it may return this transformed code for some browser targets:

```
function generateLinkTags() {
  var cssFiles = arguments.length > 0 &&
  arguments[0] !== undefined ? arguments[0] : ["/
  css/global.css"];
  return cssFiles.map(function (cssFile) {
    return "<link rel=\"stylesheet\" href=\"".
  concat(cssFile, "\">");
  }).join("");
}
```

It's an ugly transform, but most developers don't read transformed code—and therein is the point! It's precisely *because* we don't read transformed code that its cost can escape our notice. Transforming default parameters adds extra code for the sake of the developer's experience, and the cost is incurred for every default parameter added.

If needed, we could sidestep the modern syntax in favor of a legacy one:

```
function generateLinkTags (cssFiles) {
  cssFiles = cssFiles || ["/css/global.css"];

  return cssFiles.map(cssFile => {
    return '<link rel="stylesheet" href="${cssFile}">';
  }).join("");
}
```

Using the || operator, we can assign the value of `cssFiles` back to itself if its value is not `undefined`. This gives `cssFiles` a default value without requiring a transform.

"Well, that's nitpicky as hell, Jeremy." Yeah, I get it. Sometimes you want to balance maintainability more in your favor, and that's fair—but other kinds of transforms get even hairier. Take this native `fetch` wrapper that calls a local API to get JSON data from an endpoint:

```
async function fetchApiData (endpoint, param) {
  try {
    const response = await fetch('/
  api/${endpoint}/${param}');
    const data = await response.json();

    return data;
  } catch (error) {
    return error;
  }
}
```

You might notice that this wrapper is an `async` function. `async` functions are a type of function that simplifies handling promises within them by allowing one to `await` a promise rather than dealing with `then`/`catch` callback chains. They're a heck of an improvement to the developer experience, but when transformed in certain environments, they get *big* (**FIG 5.4**).

If you can't read the code in the figure, that's the point. There's too much transform bloat to be able to print it without eating up a ton of page space.

The way to get around this transform is to deal with promises directly rather than relying on `async`/`await`:

```
function fetchApiData (endpoint, param) {
  return new Promise ((resolve, reject) => {
    fetch('/api/${endpoint}/${param}').then(response
  => {
      return response.json();
    }).then(data => {
```

NAVIGATING TOOLCHAINS

```
      resolve(data);
    });
  }).catch(error => {
    reject(error);
  });
}
```

Here, we can ensure that `async`/`await` syntax doesn't add gobs of extra JavaScript to production code by using the underlying mechanism that `async`/`await` relies on.

And hey, *look*: I'm not saying never *ever* use these features otherwise you're a slop bucket of a human being. I'm just asking you to entertain the notion that tooling decisions can affect people who end up on the business end of whatever we slap up on the web. These decisions will come down to what browsers you must support, and if you can use certain features (e.g., `async`/`await`) without having to transform them for production.

It's also worth mentioning that the landscape may well have changed significantly by the time you read this. Yet, one thing will be true for some time to come: JavaScript is evolving. As long as that's the case, transpilers will be relevant. It pays to stay up to date on transpiler documentation. To wit: Babel has a concept called "compiler assumptions," which guides Babel to transform code in a way that's more efficient for your project (http://bkaprt.com/rjs39/05-12).

It takes consistent and critical evaluation of the browsers people are using to access your website. JavaScript is continually evolving, so transpilers—whether Babel, existing alternatives, or those yet to be realized—aren't going away soon. Stay vigilant, and keep an eye on what they do.

Avoid transforming early-stage features in production

Speaking of new JavaScript features, each one gets evaluated by the TC39 committee in a series of stages (http://bkaprt.com/rjs39/05-13):

```
function asyncGeneratorStep(gen, resolve, reject, _next, _throw, key, arg) { try { var info = gen[key](arg); var value = info.value; } catch
(error) { reject(error); return; } if (info.done) { resolve(value); } else { Promise.resolve(value).then(_next, _throw); } }
function _asyncToGenerator(fn) { return function () { var self = this, args = arguments; return new Promise(function (resolve, reject) { var
gen = fn.apply(self, args); function _next(value) { asyncGeneratorStep(gen, resolve, reject, _next, _throw, "next", value); } function
_throw(err) { asyncGeneratorStep(gen, resolve, reject, _next, _throw, "throw", err); } _next(undefined); }); }; }

function fetchApiData(_x, _x2) {
  return _fetchApiData.apply(this, arguments);
}

function _fetchApiData() {
  _fetchApiData = _asyncToGenerator( /*#__PURE__*/regeneratorRuntime.mark(function _callee(endpoint, param) {
    var response, data;
    return regeneratorRuntime.wrap(function _callee$(_context) {
      while (1) {
        switch (_context.prev = _context.next) {
          case 0:
            _context.next = 2;
            return fetch("/api/".concat(endpoint, "/").concat(param));

          case 2:
            response = _context.sent;
            _context.next = 5;
            return response.json();

          case 5:
            data = _context.sent;
            return _context.abrupt("return", data);

          case 7:
          case "end":
            return _context.stop();
        }
      }
    }, _callee);
  }));
  return _fetchApiData.apply(this, arguments);
}
```

FIG 5.4: Babel's transformation of a `fetch` wrapper using `async`/`await`. The transformed code is far larger than the input.

- Stage 0: These are "strawperson" proposals, in that there's no required entrance criteria. These proposals have no support within TC39.
- Stage 1: These proposals have an identified "champion" within TC39 dedicated to its advancement. These proposals can change as they advance.
- Stage 2: These are draft proposals. At this point, the behavior of the proposed feature is well-defined, but changes may still occur.
- Stage 3: These are candidate recommendations. Proposals at this stage are lightly revised, if ever.
- Stage 4: These are proposals that become standards.

This matters because Babel is used for prototyping proposed features, a necessary part of the standardization process. The problem is that plugins for transforming proposed features are publicly available, which means they can see use in production.

While familiarizing oneself with emerging features is understandable, one can't just gloss over the detriment of using and transforming experimental features in production. *Proposed* features don't always become *standardized* features. Code written using experimental features will *always* require transpiling, which represents an unnecessary performance cost.

Never use or transform experimental features in production code. Like, ever. It carries zero user-facing benefits. This is an easy thing to avoid for Babel in particular: step lightly and do your research before using plugins or presets to transform production code if their names contain the word "stage" or "proposal" (http://bkaprt.com/rjs39/05-14).

Transforms and browser support

While transpilers smooth over many compatibility gaps, we can also configure them to selectively apply transforms according to the targeted environment. Browser compatibility determines which JavaScript features you can ship untransformed—which can help you ship less JavaScript. If a feature is supported natively in your target audience's browsers, why transform it?

ES6 classes are a good example. Browsers largely support the `class` construct (http://bkaprt.com/rjs39/05-15). Still, it's not unusual for developers to transform ES6 classes and other relatively new JavaScript features for legacy browsers—even if they don't necessarily need to support them! This represents extra code that gets shipped for no good reason.

Browserslist (http://bkaprt.com/rjs39/05-16) maps Can I Use's compatibility data to browser versions. Transpilers use this data to figure out which features should be transformed for targeted browsers.

How Browserslist works

Browserslist uses a query syntax to specify browser targets. That query is then plopped into one of a few locations where your toolchain will find it:

- In the root of your project as a `.browserslistrc` file, with queries on separate lines
- In your `package.json` file as a `browserslist` key, with the corresponding value being an array containing queries
- In your transpiler configuration (http://bkaprt.com/rjs39/05-17)

Queries themselves can be as simple as `last 2 versions`, which selects the last two versions of every browser—but don't do this. `last 2 versions` means you're transforming JavaScript to be compatible all the way to Internet Explorer 10! Unless that's your intent, you're better off with a different query (http://bkaprt.com/rjs39/05-18).

If you don't specify a query, a "safe" default kicks in that transforms your JavaScript to safely run everywhere. Given that most browsers currently in use understand many modern language features (http://bkaprt.com/rjs39/05-19), that's not a good way for today's performance-minded web developer to roll.

If the default Browserslist query is no good, then what does a good query look like? Depends on the project. What browsers do your visitors use? Once you can figure that out, you'll have a shot at transforming your code in a way that's both better for performance *and* compatible with the browsers your visitors use.

A Browserslist query that works for you

If you use Google Analytics, you can feed up to thirty days of visitor data into Can I Use, which will identify the browsers your visitors use. On that website, open the settings dialog and find the "Add from Analytics" section (**FIG 5.5**):

After importing data, you'll receive a high-level overview of what browsers your website visitors use. Once you've finished, Can I Use will also contextualize feature support at the visitor level (**FIG 5.6**).

Knowing this can help you determine the right Browserslist query. For example, Legendary Tones is a website I maintain for a writer who blogs about guitars, guitar accessories, and custom amplifier modifications. He has a large readership across

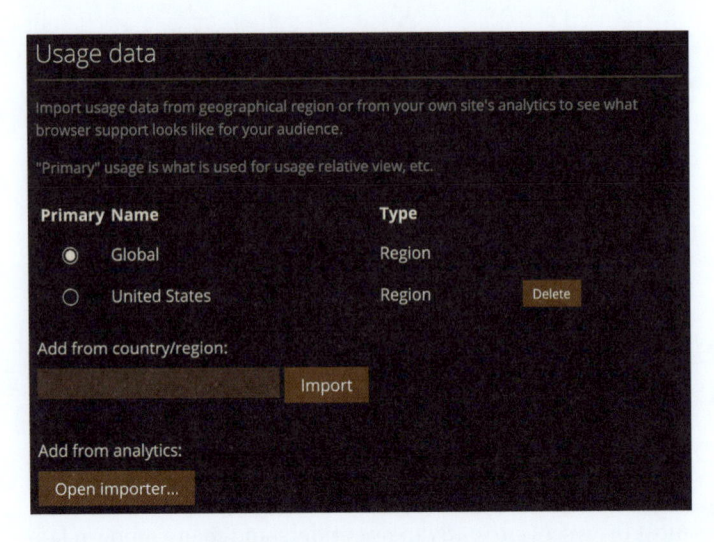

FIG 5.5: Within this dialog on the Can I Use website, there's an "Add from analytics" section where you can import Google Analytics data for a specific website.

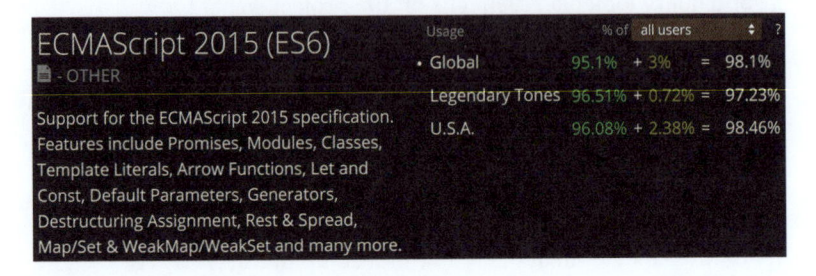

FIG 5.6: When Can I Use imports Google Analytics data for a given website, the percentage of support for a feature will also be scoped to that data.

many countries, so the browsers his readers use are diverse. Unfortunately, this means a not-insignificant share of visitors use Internet Explorer 11. To accommodate legacy browsers, I use a Browserslist query of `ie 11`.

Be aware that browser usage changes in any cohort over time. If it's not reasonable to periodically reassess support data on the Can I Use website, you may prefer to use a command line

126 RESPONSIBLE JAVASCRIPT

solution instead. browserslist-ga (http://bkaprt.com/rjs39/05-20) is one such package that can bring your analytics data directly into your toolchain.

Unfortunately, you may find that there's no single Browserslist query that strikes the proper balance between performance and compatibility. You may have just enough people using legacy browsers to keep you from transforming fewer features, but still want to find a way to avoid sending those transforms to those on modern browsers.

Lucky for you, there's a way to do just that.

INTELLIGENT BUNDLING AND DELIVERY

Here's a hair-puller of a situation: A good chunk of your website's visitors use browsers that natively support modern JavaScript features. Yet, there's this small but not insignificant portion of people on browsers that don't. You've got options:

1. You *could* just serve untransformed JavaScript using new language features to the vast majority of those on modern browsers, and accept that those on legacy browsers will have a degraded or even broken experience.
2. You could flip the script and adopt an untransformed legacy syntax when writing your JavaScript source code. That way, it'll be compatible everywhere you need it to be without a transpiler (though this also means avoiding all the new and shiny stuff). In fact, this is what GOV.UK did as late as 2021, as roughly 2 percent of their visitors in the first half of 2021 were still on some version of Internet Explorer (http://bkaprt.com/rjs39/05-21).
3. You could use all the modern language features and compile your source into two sets of bundles—one for legacy browsers and one for modern ones—and then serve them based on browser capabilities. This is called *differential serving*.

The first option can get dicey: what exactly constitutes "modern" browsers? Does your definition align with the features you're using in JavaScript? Do those features have broad support in those browsers? What happens to the visitors whose browsers aren't as "modern" as you thought? You're drawing a line in the sand that could exclude more people than you intended.

The second option is safer *and* it's more inclusive than the first—but it requires you to put your fervent desires to use the new and shiny stuff on the back burner to deliver a more broadly compatible experience. For reference, the A11Y Project mandates in their technology statement that they purposely use pre-ES6 syntax (http://bkaprt.com/rjs39/02-09) to avoid transpilers altogether. This is a valid approach that deserves careful consideration. It reduces reliance on ever-changing tooling and maximizes compatibility.

Depending on what browsers you need to support, either of the first two options may suffice. In situations where you must support browsers with fewer features, but don't want to ship a lot of extra transforms for those that do, the third option, differential serving, makes more sense. It's not as simple as the first two options, but it may be just what you need in select scenarios. Let's give it a look.

Compiling two sets of bundles

The hardest part of differential serving is setting up your toolchain to generate two sets of bundles. How it's done depends on what bundler and transpiler you use, but the toolchain architecture will generally be the same (**FIG 5.7**).

No matter what your bundler or transpiler choices are, you'll need to make sure your toolchain is structured accordingly:

1. Your transpiler will need to export two configurations: one with a Browserslist query targeting legacy browsers, and another targeting modern browsers. In the latter case, Babel's preset-env provides an `esmodules` option in its `targets` configuration (http://bkaprt.com/rjs39/05-22).
2. Your bundler will also require two separate configurations, each referencing their respective transpiler configuration. Multiple configurations can be passed in an array to the

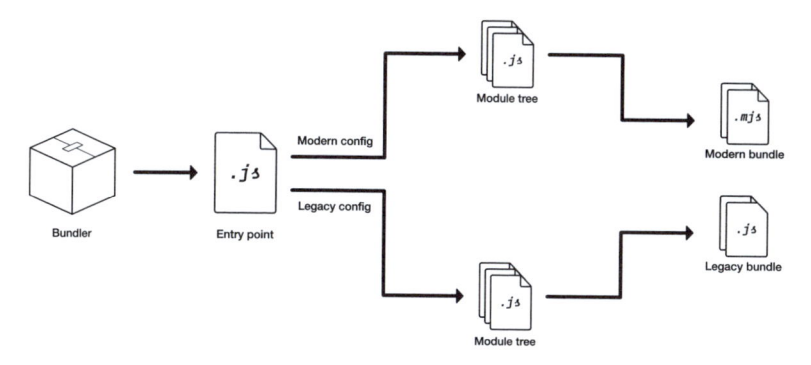

FIG 5.7: For differential serving, the bundler outputs two sets of bundles from the same entry point using two different configurations. One configuration applies minimal transforms for modern browsers, resulting in smaller bundles. The other applies all necessary transforms for legacy browsers, resulting in larger bundles.

---

bundler—this approach works with bundlers such as webpack and Rollup.

Both of these tasks take some effort to complete, and the particulars are too numerous to document in this space. For specifics, you can reference a guide I wrote on how to do this for webpack (http://bkaprt.com/rjs39/05-23), as well as a live coding demonstration (http://bkaprt.com/rjs39/05-24). I also have an example repository available (http://bkaprt.com/rjs39/05-25).

The gains you'll get from this bundling strategy depend on the project. If you're using newer features that require transforms for legacy browsers, you might see gains to the tune of 30 to 50 percent, with those on modern browsers downloading significantly less JavaScript (**FIG 5.8**). There's also an adjacent opportunity to ship fewer polyfills in your modern bundles, since targeted browsers support them natively.

If you pulled off this much, that's a big deal. It's no small thing to bifurcate your production JavaScript assets to cater to both legacy and modern browsers—but you're only halfway there. You'll still need to construct markup in order to serve these bundles to the correct browsers.

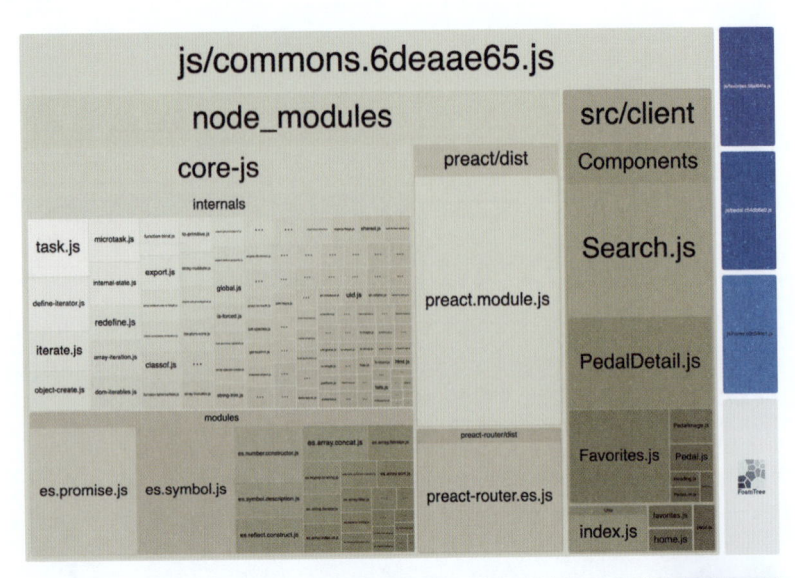

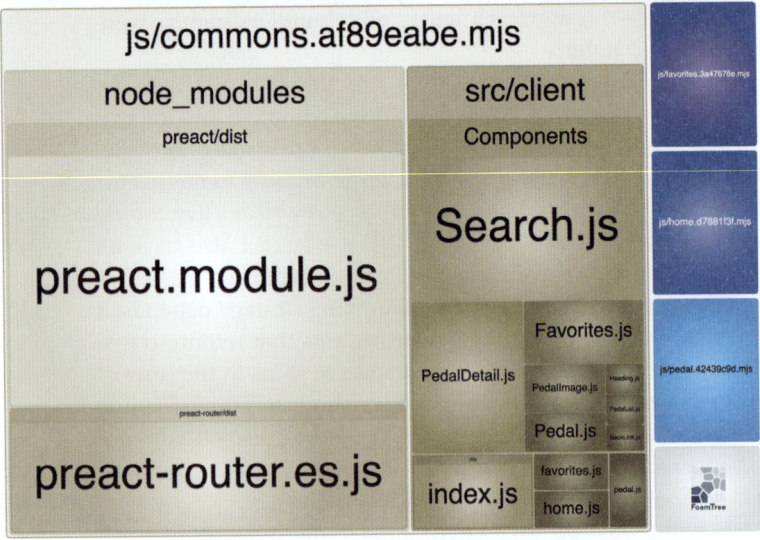

FIG 5.8: Two visualizations of a project's webpack bundle. The top bundle includes transforms and polyfills required for legacy browsers and comes in at 68.48 KiB. The bottom bundle requires little to none of those things and is 60 percent smaller at 26.75 KiB.

The module/nomodule pattern

We don't think much about the `<script>` element. We slap in an `src`, maybe tinker with `defer` or `async` attributes, and get rolling. When we bundle and serve two different versions of our JavaScript, though, there's a new approach that demands our attention: the `module`/`nomodule` pattern.

This pattern offers two parallel ways to serve JavaScript:

1. We can target browsers that support ESM—and by association, a host of other modern JavaScript language features—by setting the `<script>` element's `type` attribute value to `module`.
2. We can indirectly target browsers that don't support ESM and other modern features by applying an attribute of `nomodule` on `<script>` elements.

We can then combine these two patterns:

```
<!-- Serve modern bundles -->
<script type="module" src="/js/app.mjs"></script>
<!-- Serve legacy bundles -->
<script nomodule defer src="/js/app.js"></script>
```

This achieves the goal of differential serving by relying on two standardized behaviors:

1. Browsers won't download scripts with `type` attribute values they don't recognize. In this case, modern browsers will download scripts served with a `type` attribute value of `modern`, but legacy browsers won't.
2. Inversely, legacy browsers don't recognize the `nomodule` attribute, so they'll download scripts that use it. However, modern browsers *do* recognize `nomodule`, so they'll skip scripts with that attribute.

Even so, some browsers don't get this pattern right. Some browsers have issues where both bundles are downloaded. Some even execute both bundles (http://bkaprt.com/rjs39/05-26). You have options, though:

1. Because browsers that don't follow this pattern correctly will eventually fade out of use, you might find these suboptimizations acceptable.
2. If double-fetching of scripts for even a tiny sliver of your website's visitors isn't acceptable, you can rely on a script-injection pattern that checks for browser support of the `<script>` element's `nomodule` attribute (http://bkaprt.com/rjs39/05-27).
3. If neither option is acceptable, you could opt for a server-side approach. One method relies on user agent sniffing via the browserslist-useragent package (http://bkaprt.com/rjs39/05-28), which itself relies on Can I Use's compatibility data (http://bkaprt.com/rjs39/05-29).

Each has a drawback. The first approach means that a shrinking minority of people will incur a performance penalty—though that disadvantage is continually diminishing over time.

The second approach sidesteps the browser's preload scanner, which is a browser performance optimization that looks ahead to discover and fetch resources in the document (http://bkaprt.com/rjs39/05-30).

The third approach is best if you can't accept the risks inherent in the others. However, you may not always have an application backend, or even one that can leverage Can I Use's compatibility data. Still, if you can make it work, this approach eliminates some of these edge cases.

However you settle on differential serving, the outcome is that less JavaScript gets sent to a big chunk of your website's visitors. That translates into reduced startup time, and, in turn, makes for a better user experience. There's nothing sweeter than that.

PROCEED WITH CAUTION

Knowing how to use toolchains is equally as important as knowing *when* to use them. Failing to make this distinction may steepen a project's learning curve, which can be cumbersome when developers are excited to jump in and contribute to a project (rather than bikeshedding over the nuts and bolts of its toolchain). Approach modern tooling with healthy skepticism, but note that skepticism also has practical limits: when simpler workflows become cumbersome, it's time to pivot.

By understanding how tooling affects your website's performance, you can minimize potential damage to your user experience. This will prove especially useful as you begin to address runtime performance issues caused by JavaScript in your projects, since reducing main-thread noise will make opportunities for improvement even more apparent.

6 SMOOTHER RUNTIME PERFORMANCE

WASPS HAVE ACUTE SENSES derived from several sensory organs. Of special interest are three eyes on the top of their head called *ocelli*, set between their compound eyes (**FIG 6.1**).

Ocelli aren't compound eyes, but simple eyes that only perceive light. Entomologists hypothesize that ocelli allow wasps to sense the horizon so they can maintain a level flying path.

We've talked a lot about loading versus runtime performance. If my wasp analogy holds, you might think of loading performance as being what it takes to get off the ground—that is, starting up a web page—whereas runtime performance is what it takes to keep stable during flight—or keeping things smooth after startup.

Good runtime performance is a tall order, especially in complex architectures—but it's possible! It challenges you to think about which behaviors are best delegated to HTML and CSS, rather than using JavaScript as the sole hammer for every nail-type problem. Think about main-thread functionality in terms of which tasks are critical, which tasks can take a back seat, and which tasks you can offload to other threads altogether.

FIG 6.1: The head of a European hornet showing compound eyes with ocelli (simple eyes) between them. Photograph by Holger Casselmann (http://bkaprt.com/rjs39/06-01), CC BY-SA 3.0 (http://bkaprt.com/rjs39/06-02), via Wikimedia Commons.

LEANING MORE ON CSS AND HTML

Allow me to sit on this chair backward and rap with you for a second, fellow kids: if you want your website to be faster, using HTML and CSS in lieu of JavaScript where you can isn't a bad start. It helps to think of the web as a triumvirate of these technologies, rather than "JavaScript" and "that other stuff."

Our collective fervency for JavaScript is at a fever pitch, to the point that our appetite for CSS and HTML is dwindling by comparison. When we fail to weigh the suitability of each of the web's core technologies, we can't accurately assess which technologies are best for specific problems.

FIG 6.2: An example of a fully responsive Grid Layout that automatically flows elements based on viewport width.

Rekindling CSS

CSS is more mature and capable than it has ever been. With the advent of modern CSS layout modes such as Grid Layout and Flexbox, bespoke layouts require less code and are easier to write than ever.

To wit: I whipped up a Codepen example that demonstrates how to create a Grid Layout-powered presentation that automatically flows elements in empty spaces (http://bkaprt.com/rjs39/06-03). The markup consists of a `<ul>` element packed with `<li>` elements containing images of wasps (**FIG 6.2**). The `<ul>` itself is styled thus:

```
ul {
  display: grid;
  grid-gap: 1rem;
```

```
  grid-auto-flow: dense;
  max-width: 72rem;
  margin: 0 auto;
  grid-template-columns: repeat(auto-fit,
  minmax(12rem, 1fr));
  grid-auto-rows: 12rem;
}
```

If you're not familiar with Grid Layout, these rules are slicker than you realize. On all devices, it creates a fully responsive Grid Layout that follows these rules:

- Each row of the `<ul>` will contain as many columns as it can accommodate at the current viewport width.
- Each column will be, at a minimum, 192 pixels (`12rem`) in width, but expand up to a proportional size of one fractional unit (http://bkaprt.com/rjs39/06-04).
- Rows will be automatically added as needed, with each row being 192 pixels (`12rem`) in height. Additionally, new items will be densely packed in wherever they can fit by way of the `grid-auto-flow: dense;` rule.

We'll then spice up the layout with an `:nth-child` selector on the `<ul>` element's `<li>` children at screen sizes wider than 448 pixels (`28rem`) containing two more Grid Layout properties to give things a bit more zazz:

```
@media screen and (min-width: 28rem) {
  li:nth-child(4n + 4) {
    grid-column: span 2;
    grid-row: span 2;
  }
}
```

Zazz aside, this is pure CSS! There's no reason to reach for canned layout solutions that ship more CSS than necessary—which, let's face it, if you're shipping more CSS, you've got less headroom for more JavaScript. Grid Layout is also well

FIG 6.3: The CSS Grid Layout-powered landing page of Jen Simmons's layout lab (http://bkaprt.com/rjs39/06-06) as shown on a large screen.

supported (http://bkaprt.com/rjs39/06-05). Better yet, it won't limit you to simple layouts (FIG 6.3).

If you want to build truly eye-catching layouts that push the boundaries of what we're used to seeing on the web, CSS frameworks abstract too many of CSS's features and complex selectors away from you to take full advantage of them. For further reading on modern CSS layout modes, check the Resources section.

Lazy loading, now brought to you by HTML

Lazy loading is *the* performance pattern for the ages. It not only conserves bandwidth, but it also reduces bandwidth contention for other critical assets at startup—including JavaScript!

In the long history of the web, lazy loading has largely been a task for JavaScript. We don't need JavaScript to do this in most cases nowadays, since HTML itself provides a way to lazy-load assets referenced by `<img>` and `<iframe>` elements. Which is good, because the potential downsides of JavaScript-driven lazy loading are legion:

- Inevitably, all JavaScript-based lazy loaders require main-thread time.
- You need `<noscript>` fallback markup if users have JavaScript turned off. This adds a lot of extra bytes to your markup (http://bkaprt.com/rjs39/06-07).
- Beyond the fact that some people might have JavaScript turned off, some networks or browser plugins might block JavaScript—or your lazy loader may just fail to load altogether.
- Images—lazy-loaded or not—require `width` and `height` attributes on `<img>` elements to prevent layout shifting. If you forget to do this, your site's Cumulative Layout Shift score (CLS, from Chapter 3) may suffer.
- Lazy-loaded media won't be indexed by search engines unless you think to check for search engines (http://bkaprt.com/rjs39/06-08).

There's too much involved with JavaScript-driven lazy loading to assume every community solution will get it right. Mercifully, you can lazy-load `<img>` and `<iframe>` elements solely through HTML via the `loading` attribute's `lazy` value:

```
<!-- <img> example -->
<img src="quokka.jpg" loading="lazy" alt="A happy
  quokka.">

<!-- <iframe> example -->
<iframe src="quokka.html" loading="lazy"></iframe>
```

In this example, browsers that support native lazy loading—and a growing share of them do (http://bkaprt.com/rjs39/06-

09)—will lazy-load `quokka.jpg` for the `<img>` element and `quokka.html` for the `<iframe>` element.

Better yet, because browsers can assess network conditions, they can change loading behavior according to network quality. If the current connection is fast and stable, browsers may decide to lazy-load resources.

Worried about browsers that don't support native lazy loading? You have two options:

1. Hybrid lazy loading. This is a (sort of) polyfill that amounts to looking for the `loading` attribute in the `<img>` or `<iframe>` HTML elements. What happens next depends on the lazy-loading library you use (http://bkaprt.com/rjs39/06-10).
2. Treat native lazy loading as a progressive enhancement. This means you accept the fact that nonsupporting browsers will load images regardless of their visibility in the viewport, while supporting browsers will lazy-load them. It's imperfect, but it's simpler, and will be an increasingly viable approach as support grows.

The benefits of delegating lazy loading solely to HTML can't be understated. By relying on HTML to do something we've commonly relied on JavaScript for, both loading and runtime performance improve. Not only is relying on HTML to lazy-load simpler overall, it's more sustainable. Less work means you can turn your attention to harder problems. That's a win.

OBSERVE THIS

Various observer APIs follow a similar pattern to observe changes in certain aspects of a page: they observe a target—a DOM node, for example—and run a callback function whenever they detect change(s) in that target.

Observer APIs are worth learning because they replace the antipatterns of yore where we did wasteful stuff like, say, constantly polling for an element's visibility every time the user scrolls. Observers turn expensive work into cheap work (**FIG 6.4**).

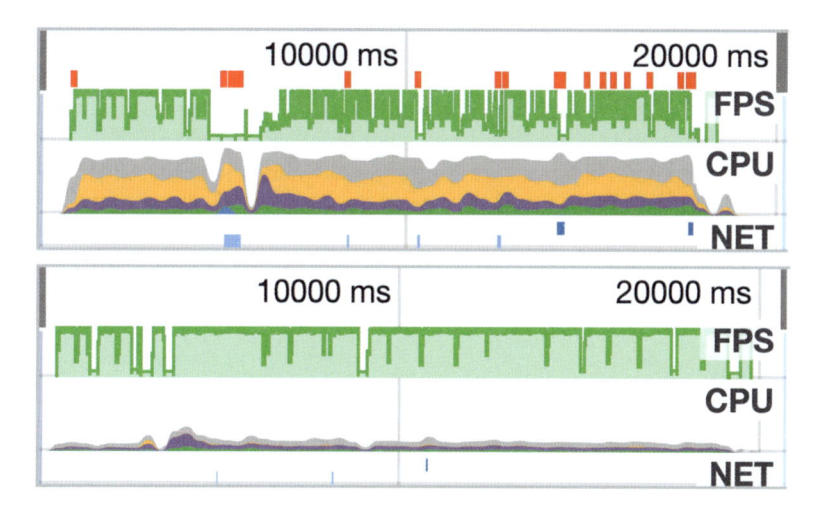

FIG 6.4: The top summary shows a page using scroll event handlers to lazy-load media. The bottom shows a page doing the same task, but using Intersection Observer instead. The latter case incurs less main-thread work, improving the framerate.

Speaking of checking for element visibility, let's start with that. Sometimes you need JavaScript to tell you if something is in the viewport. One common example of using the Intersection Observer API is lazy-loading media.

"But," you insist, "you *just* said that HTML already handles this!" It sure does! But only for `<iframe>` and `<img>` elements, which aren't the only things you *could* lazy-load. What about placeholder images for `<video>` elements?

```html
<video width="500" height="257" poster="cats-being-
  jerks.jpg">
  <source src="cats-being-jerks.webm" type="video/
  webm">
  <source src="cats-being-jerks.mp4" type="video/
  mp4">
</video>
```

If you're unfamiliar with `<video>` image placeholders, this is how they work: if you have a video that doesn't play auto-

SMOOTHER RUNTIME PERFORMANCE **141**

matically, you point its `poster` attribute to an image that will display until the video is played.

Say you have an article with a bunch of inline videos with placeholder images—that's a fair bit of data right there. You can lazy-load video `poster` images by swapping the `poster` attribute for an equivalent `data-` attribute, which contains the URL of the placeholder image to be loaded:

```
<video width="500" height="257" data-poster="cats-
  being-jerks.jpg">
```

The rest of the work involves the Intersection Observer API, which, for this use case, looks something like this:

```
const videoObserver = new
  IntersectionObserver((entries, observer) => {
  entries.forEach(entry => {
    if (entry.isIntersecting || entry.
  intersectionRatio) {
      const video = entry.target;

      video.setAttribute("poster", video.dataset.
  poster);
      video.removeAttribute("data-poster");
      observer.unobserve(video);
    }
  });
});

const videos = document.
  querySelectorAll("video[data-poster]");

videos.forEach(video => {
  videoObserver.observe(video);
});
```

Here's what's going on in the snippet:

1. We create an `IntersectionObserver` instance and assign it to a variable named `videoObserver`.
2. The `IntersectionObserver` instance takes a callback as an argument. The callback has two arguments: first, the collection of visibility changes detected—our `<video>` elements, in this case—and second, the `IntersectionObserver` instance itself.
3. Within the callback, we loop over the entries. If it's found that any of the `<video>` elements are currently in the viewport, we read the final image URL from the `data-poster` attribute and populate the element's `poster` attribute with it. Afterward, we tell the `IntersectionObserver` instance to stop observing the element.
4. We then select all `<video>` elements with a `data-poster` attribute, and then tell the newly created `IntersectionObserver` instance to observe them for changes.

With this code, we're left with a lazy-loading solution that puts grueling work where it belongs: in the browser's internals, where that work can be done more efficiently.

This is a simplistic (but effective!) Intersection Observer example. Intersection Observer can monitor changes in a variety of ways, including having its scope of observation restricted, observing partial visibility of elements, and more (http://bkaprt.com/rjs39/06-11). Its potential utility is huge; if you can think of any situation where you'd want to monitor an element's visibility, and then perform some work when its visibility changes, Intersection Observer is the right tool for the job, and it does that job *fast*.

Intersection Observer isn't the only observer in town. We also have Mutation Observer to detect if changes have occurred in the DOM, Resize Observer to detect if the size of an element has changed, and Performance Observer to detect if new entries have been added to performance APIs such as Navigation or Resource Timing. To get information on them, thumb to the Resources section at the end of the book.

OBSERVING IDLE TIME

Think of the different tasks involved in making a pizza. You might have tasks that require active and continuous focus until you're finished, like making the dough and adorning it with sauce and toppings. Then there are tasks like putting the pizza in the oven, which doesn't require your attention until it's finished baking.

The work we do in JavaScript can be similarly categorized. Actions dispatched by the user—such as opening a navigation menu or validating a form—are good examples of critical tasks that demand immediate attention.

But tasks that aren't user-driven, like sending analytics data to a collection endpoint, don't demand immediate attention. These tasks should be deprioritized to free up more main-thread time for those that *are* critical. That's where `requestIdleCallback` comes in handy.

Wait for it: Idle callbacks

`requestIdleCallback` is like `setTimeout` in that you pass a callback function as the first parameter:

```
requestIdleCallback(() => {
  // Run this callback when the browser is idle.
});
```

Unlike `setTimeout`, though, you can optionally pass an object with a timeout value in milliseconds for the second parameter:

```
requestIdleCallback(() => {
  // Run this callback when the browser is idle,
  // but run it within the next five seconds.
}, {
  "timeout": 5000
});
```

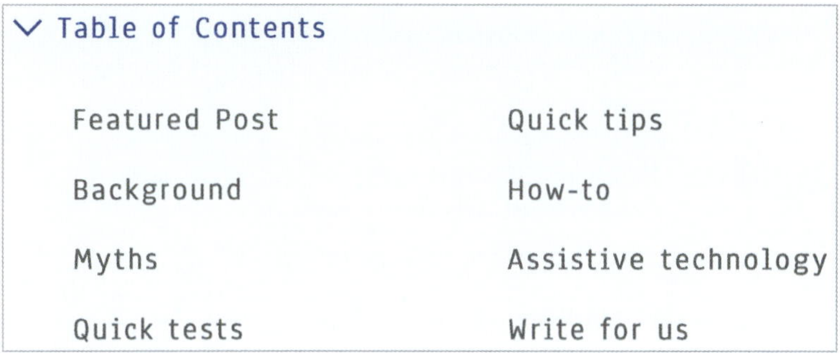

⌄ Table of Contents	
Featured Post	Quick tips
Background	How-to
Myths	Assistive technology
Quick tests	Write for us

FIG 6.5: The table of contents accordion on an article page for the A11Y Project website. Its open/closed state persists between navigations, and uses `requestIdleCallback` to ensure that managing its state doesn't interfere with other main-thread work.

Also unlike `setTimeout`, `requestIdleCallback` doesn't defer a callback's execution to a specified time in the future. The first parameter is an *idle callback,* meaning it will be executed when the main thread is idle. If a timeout is never passed to `requestIdleCallback`, then the callback runs if—and only if—the main thread is idle. If a time is specified, then the callback must run by then, or it will be run at the deadline.

There are many opportunities to use `requestIdleCallback` to defer noncritical main-thread work, but let's start simple. Every article on the A11Y Project website is accompanied by a table of contents in an accordion (**FIG 6.5**). This accordion's functionality is provided by the HTML `<summary>` and `<details>` elements.

Each page uses JavaScript to write the accordion's open/closed state to `localStorage` for return visitors (http://bkaprt.com/rjs39/04-16).

Because the accordion's open/closed state isn't reflected until someone returns to a page for which it was set, recording that state doesn't have to happen instantaneously after the user toggles it. It should be deferred to idle time to give the main thread more room to do more important work.

This calls for `requestIdleCallback`, which is what we use within the following function to set the open/closed state of the table of contents on subsequent page views:

SMOOTHER RUNTIME PERFORMANCE **145**

```
function setTOCState (detailsElement) {
  const tocStateJSON = localStorage.getItem("toc-
  state");
  const tocState = tocStateJSON === null ? [] :
  JSON.parse(tocStateJSON);
  const currentPathIndex = tocState.
  indexOf(document.location.pathname);

  if (!detailsElement.open) {
    tocState.push(document.location.pathname);
  } else if (detailsElement.hasAttribute("open") &&
  currentPathIndex !== -1) {
    tocState.splice(currentPathIndex, 1);
  }

  localStorage.setItem("toc-state", JSON.
  stringify(tocState));
}
```

This function retrieves the open/closed state from `localStorage`, which is stored in a JSON-encoded array containing path names on the site. If the current page's path name exists in the array, the table of contents will be initially closed if the page is accessed later. Otherwise, it will be open.

This function is passed as a callback to `requestIdleCallback` when the table of contents' `<details>` element is clicked:

```
const detailsElement = document.
  querySelector("details.v-toc");

detailsElement.addEventListener("toggle", () => {
  if ("requestIdleCallback" in window) {
    requestIdleCallback(() => {
      setTOCState(detailsElement);
    });

    return;
  }
```

Task
Fire Idle Callback
Function Call

FIG 6.6: The idle callback recording the visibility state of the table of contents on the A11Y Project website as shown in Chrome's performance profiler.

```
    setTOCState(detailsElement);
});
```

The `<details>` element's `toggle` event handler doesn't drive the visibility toggling for the table of contents, since we get that for free from HTML itself—but it *does* invoke `setTOCState`. Within that, we check if `requestIdleCallback` is available. If so, we pass `setTOCState` as an idle callback without a deadline (**FIG 6.6**). If `requestIdleCallback` isn't available, `setTOCState` will be run immediately.

When idle callbacks are queued without a deadline, their order is first in/first out. While this works just fine for the A11Y Project's purposes, if the page is unloaded before the idle callback runs, that work may never get done. If idle callbacks *must* run, you'll need to try a different tack.

Managing idle callbacks with urgency

Managing deadlines with `requestIdleCallback` is hard. One way to do it is to register an idle callback without a deadline, then cancel that idle callback and execute the initially deferred function immediately, if the situation is urgent.

Say you have a website that sends field data to an endpoint. Since this is low-priority work, it should never interfere with critical main-thread tasks. It may not be easy, but it's doable. To start, we'll only send data to an endpoint sometime after the window's `load` event fires. This will keep the main thread free of lower-priority work during startup.

The next part is trickier, though. Because idle callbacks without a deadline may not run if the main thread is never free, we want it to run *before* the page is unloaded. To accommodate this, we can use a function like so:

```
function urgentIdleCallback (eventOwner,
  eventString, idleCallback) {
  if ("requestIdleCallback" in window) {
    let callbackRan = false;
    const idleCallbackHandle =
  requestIdleCallback(() => {
      idleCallback();

      callbackRan = true;
    });

    eventOwner.addEventListener(eventString, () => {
      if (!callbackRan) {
        cancelIdleCallback(idleCallbackHandle);

        idleCallback();
      }
    }, {
      once: true
    });

    return;
  }

  idleCallback();
}
```

`urgentIdleCallback` takes three parameters:

1. `eventString`, which is, well, an event string (e.g., `"click"`).
2. `eventOwner`, which is the owner of the event specified in `eventString`. This is any object on which `addEventListener` is available.
3. `idleCallback`, which is the idle callback passed to `requestIdleCallback`.

With the above parameters, `urgentIdleCallback` goes through the following routine:

1. `urgentIdleCallback` first checks if `requestIdleCallback` is available. If not, `idleCallback` runs immediately.
2. We track whether the idle callback has already run in a variable named `callbackRan` which is initialized as `false`.
3. The idle callback is registered with `requestIdleCallback`, which returns a callback handle we use later if we need to cancel the idle callback. Within the idle callback, `idleCallback` will run and we'll set `callbackRan` to `true`.
4. Because the idle callback may not run right away, we register an event listener that serves as the deadline.
5. In the event's callback, we check if the idle callback has run. If not, we cancel the idle callback with `cancelIdleCallback`, which accepts the handle stored earlier in `idleCallbackHandle`. The callback then runs immediately.
6. Because we want the deadline event listener to fire just once in this case, an options object is passed to `addEventListener` with a key/value pair of `once: true`.

Now we register our urgent idle callback to run the `sendAnalytics` method, which transmits field data to a collection endpoint:

```
urgentIdleCallback(window, "pagehide",
  sendAnalytics);
```

This pattern could be used in several different situations. Just to spitball a little here, you could initialize event handlers for actions that aren't likely to be taken right away. Or you could render client-side markup for below-the-fold content.

This isn't bleeding-edge stuff. Phil Walton popularized this as the idle-until-urgent pattern (http://bkaprt.com/rjs39/06-12). Phil's approach is syntactically different from mine, but it achieves similar outcomes. He also offers a small npm package named idlize, which facilitates this pattern, including idle callback queues (http://bkaprt.com/rjs39/06-13).

Just remember one thing: Never use `requestIdleCallback` for stuff that *must* happen immediately. Idle callbacks take longer to process on slower devices. The last thing you want to do is delay critical work in environments that have less tolerance for poor performance.

`requestIdleCallback` fallbacks

Despite decent browser support, `requestIdleCallback` isn't supported everywhere (http://bkaprt.com/rjs39/06-14). While polyfills exist for `requestIdleCallback`, it can't be faithfully polyfilled because the means to do so just isn't possible in JavaScript. You'll need a fallback strategy in its absence:

- You could go the progressive enhancement route and run callbacks immediately in the absence of `requestIdleCallback`. This works, but not everyone gets the same experience. Regarding `requestIdleCallback`, I don't think that's such a bad thing—but hey, it's your website, so it's your call.
- If you *must* use `requestIdleCallback` with a deadline, one fallback could be `setTimeout`. `setTimeout` isn't apples to apples with `requestIdleCallback`, but might be worth considering (http://bkaprt.com/rjs39/06-15).
- Finally—and this is the most direct method if other strategies won't suffice—use a polyfill, but with the understanding that any polyfill of `requestIdleCallback` can't faithfully emulate a native implementation of it (http://bkaprt.com/rjs39/06-16). If you're leaning in this direction, proceed carefully. The `requestIdleCallback` polyfill is sophisticated, but it's also extra JavaScript for something that can never be faithfully replicated.

If all this idle callback business seems a bit much, then remember: it's relatively new when you consider how long the web has been a thing. Naturally, it'll take practice and exploration to learn where it can be applied. Once you take `requestIdleCallback` out for a spin, you'll be rewarded with a better user experience that prioritizes critical work. That's a nice payoff.

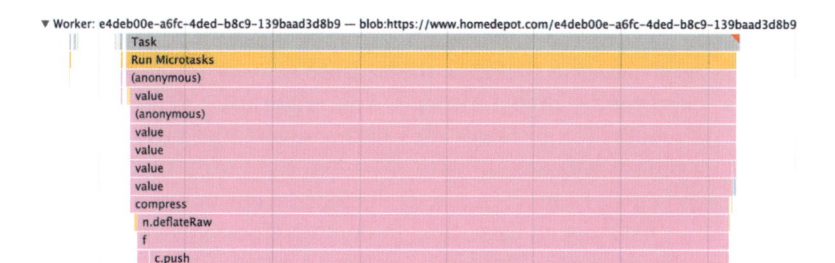

FIG 6.7: A call stack from a web worker running on its own thread on the Home Depot website as shown in Chrome's performance profiler. The tasks on this thread give the main thread breathing room to do more urgent and user-facing work.

GOING OFF THE MAIN THREAD

Think of the main thread as being like the front counter at a fast-food joint. When the whole joint's understaffed, there are not only too few employees to take orders, but also to cook the food to fulfill them. The service worsens as orders accumulate and the employees can't keep up with them. As things deteriorate, so too does the customer experience. Without adequate staff to support the front counter, service suffers.

If the front-counter staff represents the main thread, you can think of everything that supports them as something similar to a *worker thread*. Like the cooks well behind the counter, worker threads are where *web workers* can keep the main thread running smoothly when there's much work to be done (**FIG 6.7**).

While uses for web workers abound, it can be a little difficult to know exactly what you might use them for without a real-world example, so let's explore one together.

Move taxing tasks into web workers

Oft-cited examples of web workers involve fetching and processing a massive amount of data in a worker thread, and then ferrying the result to the main thread. While this is a great use case, it's not the only one.

Say you're building a photography web app where people need access to Exif data, the treasure trove of image metadata captured by digital cameras. You might use `fetch` to make a request for an image file's data, convert that raw data into a binary data stream with `ArrayBuffer` (http://bkaprt.com/rjs39/06-17), and then extract the Exif data from it.

That's not an easy thing to do, though, so you could use a package like ExifReader (http://bkaprt.com/rjs39/06-18) to process image Exif data for you. However, doing this on the main thread incurs considerable work on a few fronts:

- Loading ExifReader on the main thread
- Kicking off a `fetch` for an image asset
- Converting the image response into a blob and ultimately into an `ArrayBuffer` as well as extracting the Exif data
- Constructing markup to display the Exif data

JavaScript engines do their best to split work up into manageable chunks, but long tasks aren't always avoidable. Therefore, this work is best left to a separate thread.

To demonstrate how fetching an image from the network and extracting Exif data from it can be done by a web worker, I created a demo app named JPEG Metadata Extractor (http://bkaprt.com/rjs39/06-19) to do exactly that.

The app's repository contains two tags. The first (http://bkaprt.com/rjs39/06-20) does all the `fetch` and metadata extraction on the main thread (**FIG 6.8**). The second (http://bkaprt.com/rjs39/06-21) does all the same work as the first, only it does most of that work on a worker thread (**FIG 6.9**).

The demo app's interface accepts a JPEG URL, which is retrieved via a `fetch`. Even if we use a web worker, *some* things will still have to be done on the main thread:

- Register a `submit` event listener on the form
- Validate the form's inputs
- Pass the image URL to the web worker

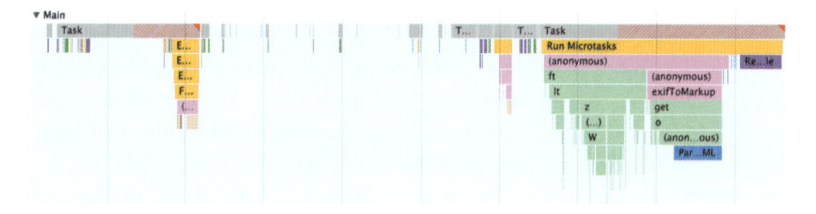

FIG 6.8: Image fetching and Exif metadata extraction as it occurs on the main thread. As a result, two long tasks occur on the main thread with a total blocking time of nearly 150 milliseconds.

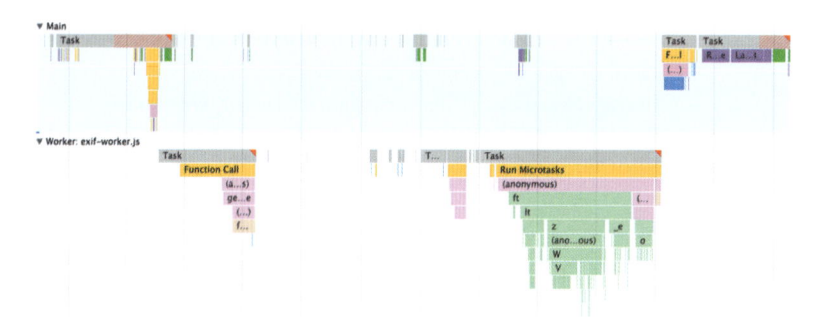

FIG 6.9: Main-thread activity (at top) and web worker activity (at bottom). While form submission and Exif markup insertion must still occur on the main thread, the image fetching and Exif extraction work occurs on a separate thread, reducing main-thread blocking time.

Almost everything after that can be done in the web worker, which resides in a separate script named `exif-worker.js`. The web worker is registered on the main thread like so:

```
const exifWorker = new Worker("/js/exif-worker.js");
```

Then, we import ExifReader using the `importScripts` function in the web worker (http://bkaprt.com/rjs39/06-22). `importScripts` accepts a URL string to import an external script to be used in the worker scope:

```
importScripts("/js/exifreader.js");
```

SMOOTHER RUNTIME PERFORMANCE **153**

In some browsers, the static `import` syntax can be used to import scripts if you register a web worker in module mode (http://bkaprt.com/rjs39/06-23). Depending on browser support, though, you might have to stick with `importScripts`.

Communicating between the main thread and a worker thread

Web workers are only useful if bidirectional communication between them and the main thread is possible. Well, whaddya know—you can do this by way of the worker's `postMessage` method (http://bkaprt.com/rjs39/06-24).

In the case of our JPEG metadata extractor, we can use `postMessage` to pass the JPEG image URL provided in the form to the worker:

```
exifWorker.postMessage(imageUrl);
```

From there, we intercept the message in the worker context through its `message` event. A `data` property within the `message` event's `event` object contains the data sent via `postMessage` from the main thread. We then feed that data into a function that fetches the image and returns the Exif data formatted in markup:

```
self.addEventListener("message", event => {
  getExifDataFromImage(event.data).then(status => {
    self.postMessage(status);
  }).catch(status => {
    self.postMessage(status);
  });
});
```

`getExifDataFromImage` returns a promise that states whether the operation was successful as well as a message. If all goes well, the message will contain the Exif data in a markup string.

The next step is to get the Exif metadata *out* of the web worker. We do that by invoking the `postMessage` method again. Only this time we send data from within the worker to the main thread.

Intercepting that message on the main thread is similar to how we intercept messages in a worker: we add a `message` event listener on the worker instance:

```
exifWorker.addEventListener("message", event => {
  // Access information passed from the worker
  // here through the event.data object.
});
```

With this bidirectional channel, we have a way to ferry data to and from web workers. The `postMessage`/`message` event pattern isn't exclusive to web workers, either—service workers can use this communication pattern too.

If this method of transferring data between workers and the main thread is cumbersome to you, there are abstractions that simplify that work. Comlink (http://bkaprt.com/rjs39/06-25) is an excellent and minimalist off-the-shelf abstraction by Surma (http://bkaprt.com/rjs39/06-26) for web worker communication.

Does it make a difference?

Yes. Any chance to shift costly tasks onto separate threads makes a difference. This was certainly the result when it came to the JPEG Metadata Extractor. Web workers can't handle *everything* the JPEG Metadata Extractor does, but they can take the grueling work off the main thread and create more headroom for other work. Now people—particularly those on low-end devices—can interact with the metadata extraction tool with less lag.

As a bonus, if you load any scripts within the web worker context, the web worker parses and compiles these off the main thread as well. If a dependency in your application can be restricted solely to the web worker scope, you can also confine its startup costs to the worker thread. That's a big deal.

What else are web workers good for?

While a web worker's scope is much narrower than the main thread's, web workers can still accomplish all sorts of computationally expensive tasks:

- They can offload processing of large amounts of data to keep the main thread clear for other work. Mapbox GL (http://bkaprt.com/rjs39/06-27) does this with loading and rendering map data to ensure that user interactions are as smooth as they can be.
- They can communicate image data to and from WASM-compiled binaries for optimization. Squoosh (http://bkaprt.com/rjs39/06-28) is a browser-based image optimization app that uses web workers this way.
- They can perform DOM updates and mutations in a web worker context. Google's experimental WorkerDOM contains an implementation of the DOM API inside of a web worker (http://bkaprt.com/rjs39/06-29).

If the work that needs to be done on your website doesn't require direct access to the DOM and is computationally expensive, web workers can improve your website's runtime performance by reducing main-thread work.

CHARTING A COURSE FOR A SNAPPIER WEB

Web performance is more than just how fast a website loads. Where JavaScript is concerned, that sentiment fails to see the whole picture. JavaScript has an equally important, if not more important, role in a website's usability *after* its load event fires.

Poor runtime performance sows distrust in your website. While that's bad for business (if business is your business), it's also bad for users. If you work on a website that serves any remotely critical function, keeping an eye on runtime performance must be a priority, especially for long-lived websites that mature and add features over time.

With a little thought and care, you can find opportunities to use the techniques covered in this chapter to make runtime performance better for more people on more devices. That work benefits everyone, everywhere. As we roll into the final stretch and touch on the pitfalls of third-party JavaScript, you're going to need all the breathing room you can get on the main thread in order to chart a course for smooth sailing.

7 MANAGING THIRD-PARTY JAVASCRIPT

IF YOU'RE LOOKING FOR PROOF of the truism that all wasps are jerks, look no further than the paper wasp species *Polistes sulcifer*, also known as the cuckoo paper wasp.

Cuckoo paper wasps look like common paper wasps (*Polistes dominula*, specifically) but with one important difference: they forgot how to build their own nests a long time ago. Rather than strike out on their own—you know, like any reasonable solitary wasp would—a fledgling female instead takes over a colony of common paper wasps through a combination of chemical mimicry and the time-tested practice of regicide (**FIG 7.1**). Once the cuckoo wasp establishes herself as the new queen, she forces the workers of the host nest to raise her offspring.

Think of your website as a happy little nest, with its various scripts and such doing their own thing. At some point, you'll probably rely on a third-party script to do something for you that you yourself don't have time to build a solution for.

One third-party script or two won't likely do tons of damage performance-wise, but make no mistake: they can insidiously creep in over time. At the very worst, they can parasitize your

FIG 7.1: A nest of *Polistes dominula* paper wasps. Females of the species *Polistes sulcifer* usurp the queens of these nests and force the remaining workers to raise their offspring. Photograph by JAW (http://bkaprt.com/rjs39/07-01), CC BY-SA 3.0 (http://bkaprt.com/rjs39/07-02), via Wikimedia Commons.

---

website and ship scripts to your users that you didn't even know about. Since you may not be able to eliminate the presence of third-party JavaScript on your website entirely, you'll need to keep a close eye on things to prevent serious performance issues from manifesting.

I'll be up-front: there's no way we can cover every pitfall you'll face with third-party JavaScript in such limited space. This subject would require its own book to completely explore. Rather, we're going to train our focus on some of the big stuff for you to consider as well as technical mitigations you can use to help rein things in.

DEFINING TERMS

Even the task of distinguishing first- and third-party JavaScript is a trudge, but I'll try my best: *first-party JavaScript* is any JavaScript we write that's specific to our website, including its dependencies. If you yourself wrote some JavaScript, or you installed dependencies with a package manager and bundled them as production-ready scripts that are served from your domain, you can usually call that first-party JavaScript.

Defining third-party JavaScript is more difficult. Some might say that third-party scripts are those loaded from any cross-origin, but that definition gets weird in cases where you load your first-party code's dependencies from public CDNs or even a subdomain of your primary origin.

For the sake of expediency, we'll define *third-party JavaScript* to mean any script from a service provider—paid or otherwise—that provides some service for a website. This may include (but certainly isn't limited to) client-side A/B testing suites, analytics and tag managers, heatmapping tools, accessibility overlays, and so on.

This isn't an exhaustive accounting of third-party products, but it should give you an idea of what third-party JavaScript encompasses conceptually—and as you'll find out, there are some seriously formidable threats in your nest where performance is concerned.

THE DEALERS OF DAMAGE

Third-party JavaScript tends to make its way into a website because it tends to bridge some gap in a website's current functionality that its owners don't want—or can't afford—to solve on their own. After all, developer time is spendy, and if a UX researcher, marketer, or product owner finds they can spend less money on a third-party solution than what it would take to develop a custom solution, they can hardly be blamed for choosing the former.

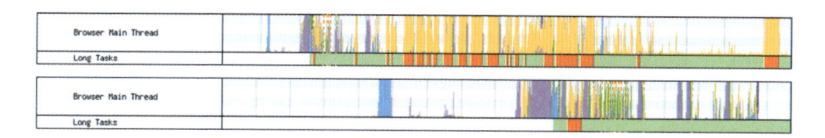

FIG 7.2: A WebPageTest comparison of main-thread activity for the Government of South Carolina's unemployment assistance information page. At the top, no requests for third-party scripts are blocked. At the bottom, all third-party scripts are blocked. Without third-party scripts, the page is still usable and informative, but incurs a fraction of the blocking time.

Adopting a third-party solution for a missing piece of functionality may feel inevitable. When that feeling is palpable across an organization, you'll do well to ask a pointed question: What purpose does this product serve? Then, an even more pointed follow-up question: Does this product hurt our goals?

Take South Carolina's landing page for their unemployment assistance information page. It's a simple informational page, yet it ships nearly three megabytes of JavaScript, which becomes ten megabytes after decompression. The lion's share of that JavaScript is wrapped up in third-party scripts, and its effects are seriously detrimental to both loading and runtime performance (FIG 7.2).

To be fair to the State of South Carolina, some of the third-party JavaScript loaded on this informational page is useful, such as YouTube embeds of informational videos. Even so, they could provide this information as outbound links that go directly to YouTube, or even load it inline as a result of a user interaction, rather than embedding it on the page willy-nilly.

On the other hand, some other third-party stuff has dubious utility—chat widgets in particular require a lot of additional and arguably unnecessary JavaScript. A good alternative is the practical one: give people a phone number or an email address. At the very least, none of the chat widget's JavaScript should ever load until someone shows intent to *use* it.

Either way, only one thing will ever be true when it comes to third-party products: page speed will be better for each one you *don't* use. This isn't to say that they're never useful, but

MANAGING THIRD-PARTY JAVASCRIPT **161**

treat every new script with healthy skepticism. While some third-party scripts can be indispensably useful for many organizations, there are \several you need to approach with a side-eye at the ready.

Client-side A/B testing frameworks

A/B testing is a form of research that evaluates how variations on design, content, or functionality affect engagement. Rather than rolling out a significant change to the live site, you show one version of The New Thing to half of your audience and show the status quo to the remainder—that's the simplest explanation, anyway (**FIG 7.3**).

A/B testing is supposed to inform decisions on evolving your product, which is an inherently good idea! However, it's usually conducted with client-side JavaScript, which carries the predictable performance outcomes:

- Testing scripts modify the DOM on the fly. This often requires the necessary JavaScript to be loaded in the document `<head>` as a render-blocking resource in order to avoid noticeable changes to the user interface.
- More JavaScript equals more problems—namely, more processing on the main thread, which disproportionately affects those on low-end devices and slower networks.
- If A/B testing solutions attach numerous event listeners to DOM elements, that can slow down runtime performance—something you just can't afford if you're already hanging off the cliff when it comes to those on low-end devices.

Assess whether the benefit of doing this research outweighs the impact, or whether its potentially negative performance impacts could skew test results. Changing page structure and presentation on the fly is a risky business, and the work to run the test can still be considerable even on capable hardware (**FIG 7.4**).

If you're conducting A/B testing, ensure your testing framework offers a server-side option, or consider switching to one that does. If you can ensure you won't skew your test results

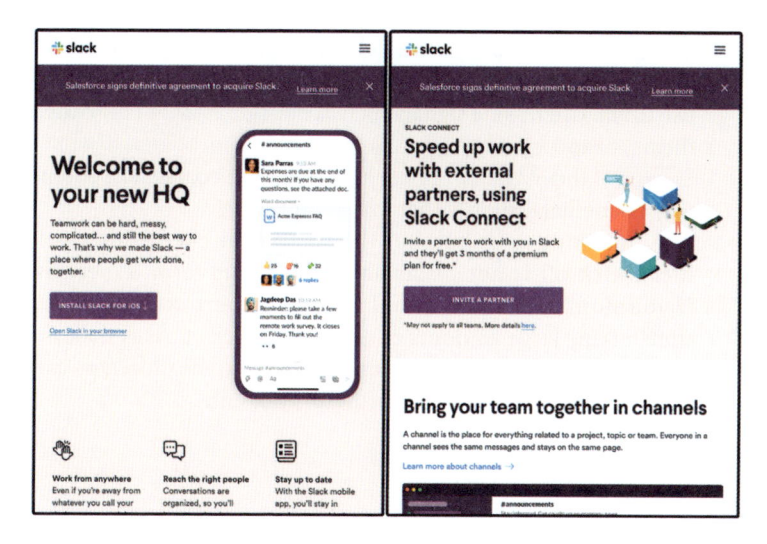

FIG 7.3: A/B testing allows organizations to evaluate multiple design and messaging variations before committing to a change.

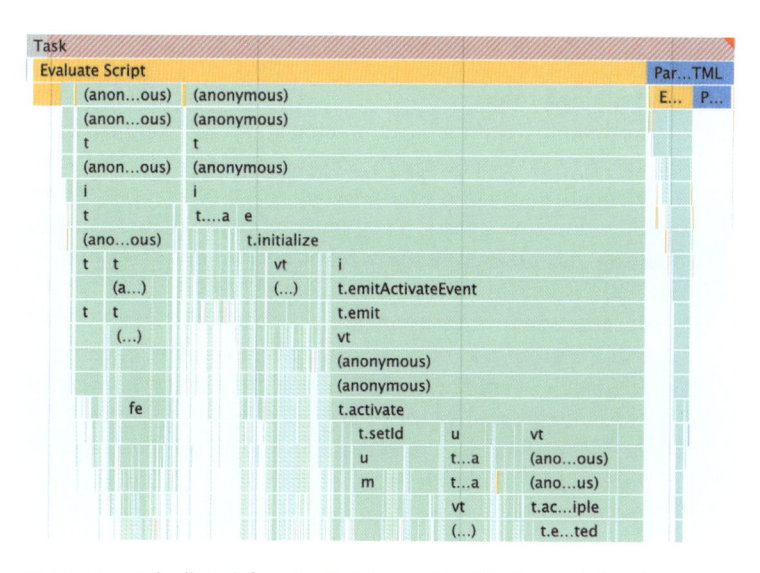

FIG 7.4: A partial call stack from the Best Buy website. This long task (roughly 225 milliseconds) was triggered by a client-side A/B testing script on the Best Buy website. The blocking portion of the task is roughly 175 milliseconds.

MANAGING THIRD-PARTY JAVASCRIPT   **163**

by doing so, consider not conducting A/B testing on low-end devices, particularly if a sizable part of your audience doesn't use them. Client-side signals such as `navigator.deviceMemory` (http://bkaprt.com/rjs39/07-03) and `navigator.hardwareConcurrency` (http://bkaprt.com/rjs39/07-04) are coarse, but potentially beneficial, signals that may help.

A/B testing is useful, but the significant client-side work it can kick off is not sustainable in the long term, especially if you don't consistently cull finished experiments to avoid transferring large amounts of unused JavaScript. As is the case with most JavaScript performance problems, the more you can offload to servers, the more browsers benefit.

Accessibility overlays

Accessibility overlays are third-party products that claim to automatically fix website accessibility issues through client-side JavaScript. Accessibility overlays are enticing because inaccessible websites carry real legal consequences (http://bkaprt.com/rjs39/07-05). Accessibility work is *tough*. It takes skilled developers and considerable time, effort, and money to fix accessibility problems.

Accessibility cannot be automated away. By using an accessibility overlay, you are tacitly admitting that your website has problems that you don't want to fix. Worst of all, accessibility overlays don't even work. They cause more problems than they fix (http://bkaprt.com/rjs39/07-06):

- In cases where `<img>` elements lack proper `alt` text, overlays will generate text. This text may be excessively verbose, effectively turning a gap of information into a burden for those using assistive technologies.
- Overlays often provide a content-scaling feature. Depending on how a website is styled, the overlay's assumptions about how to scale content may cause elements to overlap or become obscured. Properly styling your website using relative CSS units ensures your website can be properly scaled by the browser's native zoom controls.

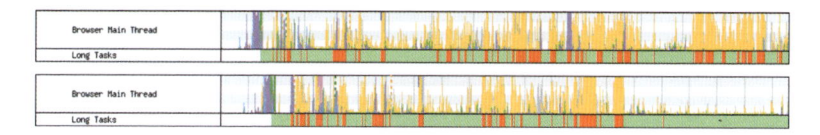

FIG 7.5: A WebPageTest comparison of the main thread of Samsung's US website with AudioEye's accessibility overlay loaded (top) and without it (bottom). AudioEye's accessibility overlay incurred more than twice as much blocking time than without it.

- Content scaling may also cause issues with readability in body copy with static `line-height` values, as scaling up content may cause lines of text to overlap and become unreadable.
- Overlays themselves may have excessive, unintuitive interactions. accessiBe's overlay product contains more than seventy-five controls, which clutter the interface and overwhelm users.

There's a lot more that can go wrong, and—*and*—on top of all that pain, performance gets worse (FIG 7.5).

Accessibility overlays are snake oil at best. They don't make your website more accessible, and they're downright poisonous for performance. When you use them, you're making things worse and throwing good money after bad.

The ethos of this book is performance-centric, but accessibility is another aspect of using JavaScript responsibly. If you need to level up your accessibility game, check out *Accessibility for Everyone* by Laura Kalbag (http://bkaprt.com/rjs39/07-07). The Resources section also has a few links that can point you in the right direction.

Heatmaps

Heatmaps visualize which parts of a page people interact with most frequently to determine the value of interface elements or layout choices. They get their name from their resemblance to thermal imaging: areas of high interaction frequency are visualized as hot, and areas of low interaction frequency as cold (FIG 7.6).

FIG 7.6: Heatmap overlays illustrate the frequency of user interactions on a scale from green ("cold") to red ("hot").

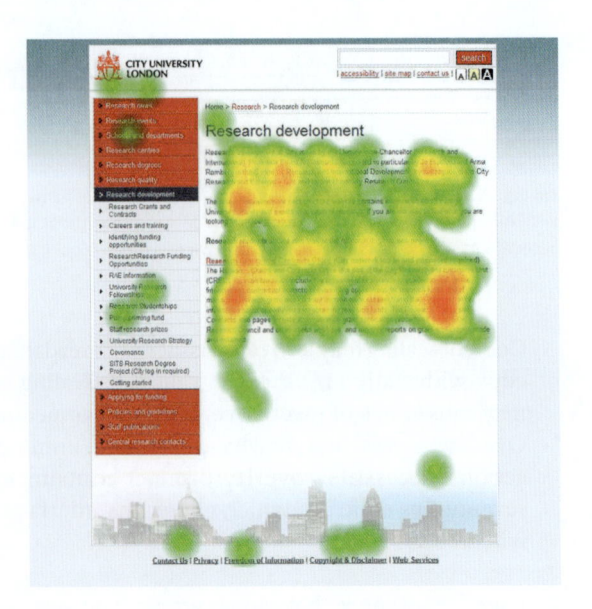

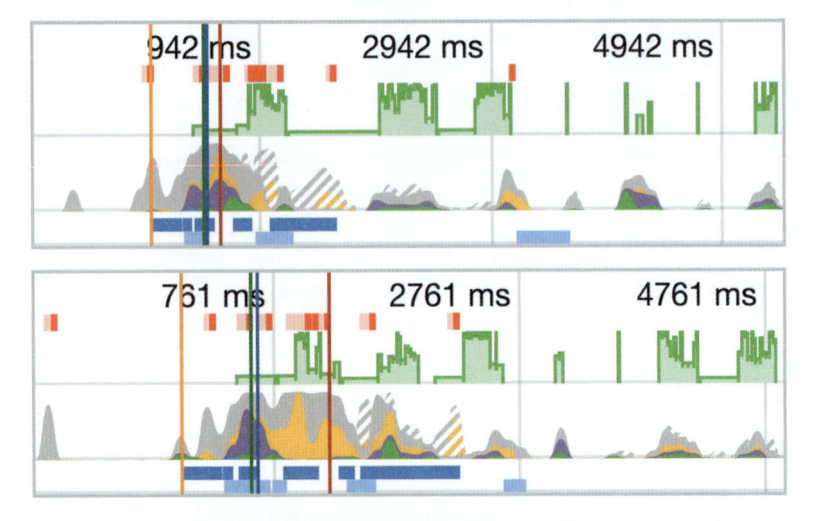

FIG 7.7: Two main-thread activity summaries of the same page profiled on a Nokia 2 Android phone. The top summary is of a page without any third-party scripts. The bottom summary is of the same page with a third-party heatmapping tool. The interactions in each session are identical, but the heatmapping tool introduces three times more JavaScript activity.

Some heatmapping tools also provide the ability to "play back" a specific visitor's session. Tracking page interactions and cursor position in order to reconstruct the playback—usually called *session replay*—chews up tons of CPU. That's a tax that's never worth levying on anyone, let alone those on low-end devices (**Fig 7.7**).

Honestly? Don't bother with heatmapping. You can gather more valuable signals on your own. For example, if you run a blog or news website and you want to know how much of your content people are reading, you can use an intersection observer to track the visibility of each element within a page's `<article>` element, and then send that data to an endpoint for later analysis.

I get it. Everything I'm saying feels all finger-pointy, and UX research is about refining the user experience—but, as Erika Hall notes in *Just Enough Research*, you can get better insights by listening to users (http://bkaprt.com/rjs39/07-08). Not only will you get better usability data, but you'll also avoid the mucky performance issues associated with heatmapping tools.

TECHNICAL MITIGATIONS

Whether you dig it or not, it's likely a website you work on will ship one or more third-party products. This doesn't mean your website's user experience is doomed! It just means you should try to mitigate the impact of those third-party scripts.

Self-hosting revisited

Remember when we covered self-hosting in Chapter 4? It's back! To recap, you can improve loading performance by eliminating sources of connection latency. In the same fashion, self-hosting third-party assets will speed things up.

Unfortunately, self-hosting third-party scripts isn't always possible. Any third-party script with contents that regularly or unpredictably change—such as Google Analytics scripts—are a no-go for self-hosting.

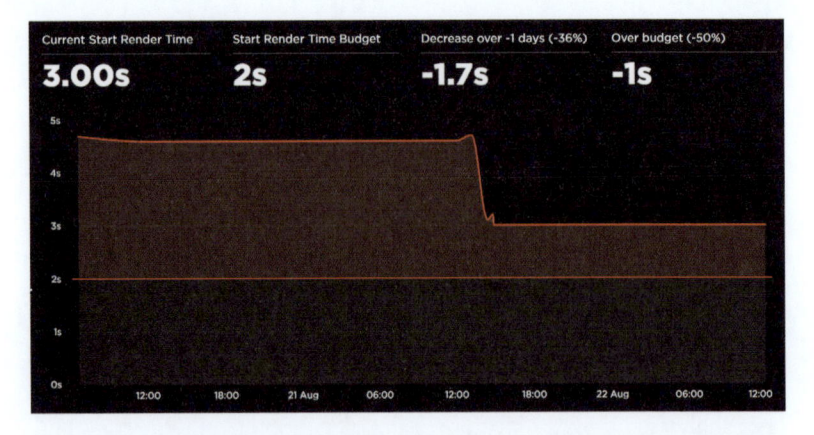

FIG 7.8: Start render time for the Casper Sleep website in SpeedCurve. Self-hosting their A/B testing framework led to a 1.7 second decrease in start render time. Chart courtesy of Kyle Rush (http://bkaprt.com/rjs39/07-11).

Don't despair! It's possible to self-host *some* third-party scripts, and to great benefit. Notably, Casper Sleep found a way in 2018 to self-host their A/B testing framework JavaScript, reducing their start render time by 1.7 seconds (http://bkaprt.com/rjs39/07-09). A/B testing frameworks must be loaded in the `<head>` in blocking fashion to avoid bad user-experience outcomes, such as flashes of unstyled content (http://bkaprt.com/rjs39/07-10). Self-hosting ended up being a crucial performance improvement in this case (**FIG 7.8**).

If a third-party vendor enables you to self-host their JavaScript, that's a sign that your website's performance is a priority to them. That goes double if you're a paying customer. Put a little friendly pressure on your third-party vendors to see whether self-hosting is a feasible accommodation.

Establish early connections

If self-hosting is off the table, establishing early connections for third-party scripts with `rel=preconnect` can mask connection latency in a big way.

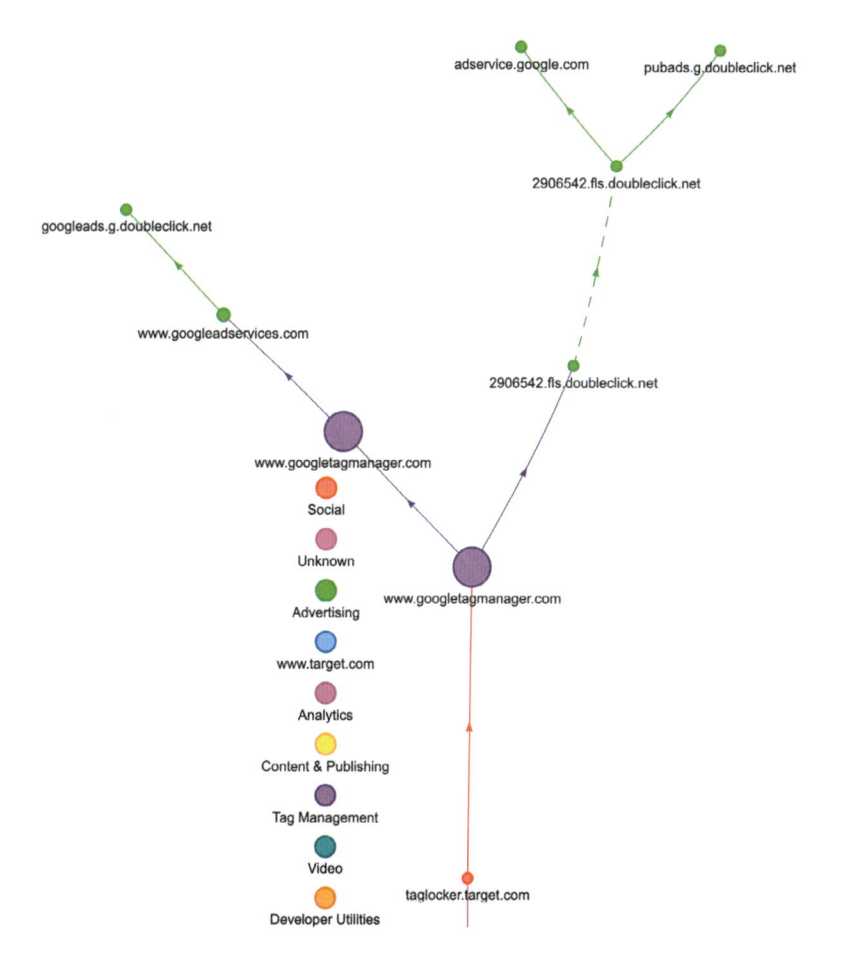

FIG 7.9: A partial visualization (via Simon Hearne's Request Map Generator) of a third-party script request chain on Target's website.

Sometimes assets loaded from third-party servers kick off these nasty *request chains* (**FIG 7.9**). A request chain is when an origin requests an asset from another origin, and so on. Request chains are terrible for performance because they introduce more latency for every new origin discovered in the request chain.

MANAGING THIRD-PARTY JAVASCRIPT

Simon Hearne's Request Map Generator (http://bkaprt.com/rjs39/07-12) finds all the unique origins involved for a given web page. You can also use the Domains tab in WebPageTest to do this. With this information, you can establish connections as early as possible using the `preconnect` resource hint, which we covered in Chapter 4. If you can avoid some of the latency involved in these request chains, that's a big performance win.

Don't preload third-party scripts

As you'll recall from Chapter 4, `preload` triggers an early fetch for resources. It's a powerful performance optimization, and you should use it sparingly, as it can help or harm in equal measure.

When you preload assets, you're effectively boosting their priority; if everything is prioritized, then nothing is. Where `preload` and JavaScript is concerned, you should only use it for first-party scripts that are critical to rendering—and that's *only* if you can't find a way to take such JavaScript out of the critical path and serve contentful markup directly from the server. In any case, squandering `preload`s on third-party scripts siphons away available bandwidth from scripts that power critical user-experience fixtures.

Users don't care if your analytics or heatmapping tools load faster. They're after your content or product. You should never prioritize gathering data over performance, so save `preload` for the stuff that provides a material user-experience benefit.

The fruits of laziness

Few of the third-party products I've referenced throughout this chapter have a direct user-experience benefit. But some *do*, such as social media sharing functionality and embedded video content. These third-party scripts are arguably more valuable than many others we've discussed thus far.

Video embedding services are especially valuable, because transcoding video to different formats and managing adaptive streaming quality is extremely hard to do. It makes perfect sense

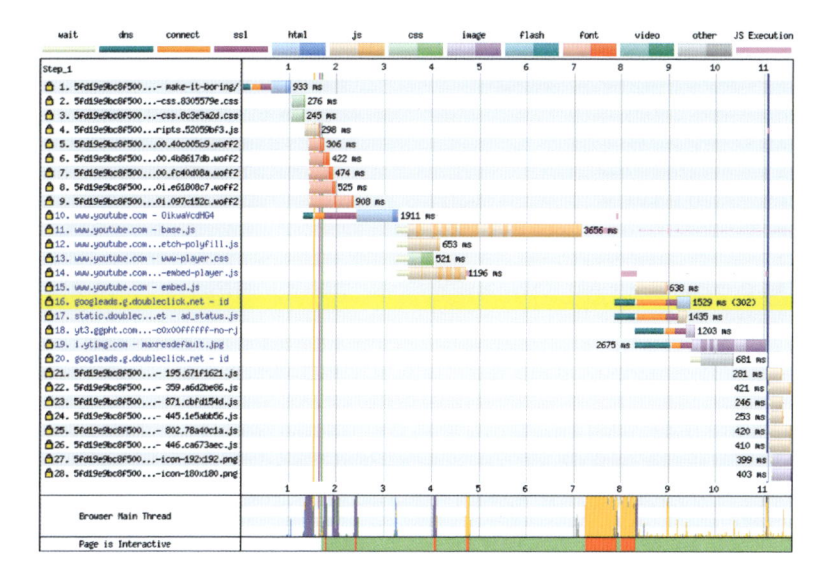

FIG 7.10: A WebPageTest waterfall view of a blog page with a YouTube `<iframe>` embed. The `<iframe>` and its assets begin on the tenth request. The embed incurs considerable main-thread blocking time when loaded.

---

to want to use these services. Unfortunately, they incur a lot of overhead beyond the necessary video payloads they deliver.

YouTube uses a lot of JavaScript in its `<iframe>` embeds (**FIG 7.10**). If you're embedding YouTube video that's "below the fold," as it were, you should lazy-load those iframes to reduce bandwidth contention and blocking time at startup (**FIG 7.11**).

You could achieve this by slapping a `loading="lazy"` attribute on the `<iframe>` or reach for an open-source solution that lazy-loads iframes in all browsers—or even some hybridized combination of the two if broad compatibility is needed.

However, not all third-party embedded content is provided by iframes. This means that lazy-loading JavaScript can get more complicated for other types of embeds. Take Facebook's Like button embed, which consists of two parts. The first part is an HTML placeholder for the button:

MANAGING THIRD-PARTY JAVASCRIPT

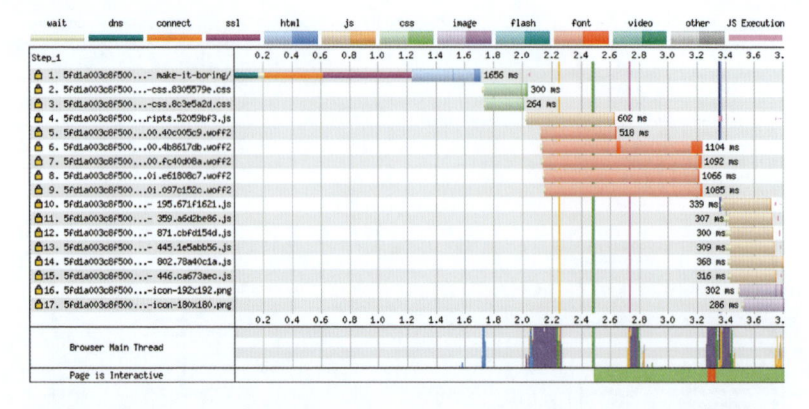

FIG 7.11: A WebPageTest waterfall view of the same blog page with the YouTube embed's `<iframe>` element using the `loading="lazy"` attribute. The content won't load until it approaches the viewport, freeing up valuable bandwidth and system resources during startup.

```
<div class="fb-like" data-href="https://developers.
  facebook.com/docs/plugins/" data-width="" data-
  layout="standard" data-action="like" data-
  size="small" data-share="true"></div>
```

The second part is a small HTML snippet and a Facebook-provided `<script>` tag:

```
<div id="fb-root"></div>
<script async defer crossorigin="anonymous"
  src="https://connect.facebook.net/en_US/sdk.
  js#xfbml=1&version=v9.0"></script>
```

Facebook's JavaScript embed is *honkin'* big. The script referenced in the snippet above is over 700 kilobytes uncompressed! Avoid it altogether if you can, but chances are that if you're already in this situation, you can't. If that's the case, your best option is to mitigate the damage. Unless the Like button is at the top of the page, it's not worth the extra processing to load Facebook's giant chunk of JavaScript during startup, where it will compete with other resources. An intersection observer helps us out here:

```
const intersectionListener = new
  IntersectionObserver(([ entry ], observer) => {
  if (entry.isIntersecting || entry.
  intersectionRatio) {
    const scriptEl = document.
  createElement("script");

    scriptEl.defer = true;
    scriptEl.crossOrigin = "anonymous";
    scriptEl.src = "https://connect.facebook.net/
  en_US/sdk.js#xfbml=1&version=v9.0";

    document.body.append(scriptEl);
    observer.disconnect();
  }
});

intersectionListener.observe(document.
  querySelector(".fb-like"));
```

This code snippet does the following:

1. A new `IntersectionObserver` instance is created. In its callback, we only need the first entry in the entry list since we're only observing the visibility of a single `div.fb-like` element.
2. Once the element is in viewport, a new `<script>` element is created with the `document.createElement` method (http://bkaprt.com/rjs39/07-13).
3. With the `<script>` element created, we assign three attributes to it: its cross-origin request type (`anonymous`), whether to defer its execution, and its `src`. We then append it to the bottom of the `<body>`.
4. Once all that's done with, we call the observer's `disconnect` method to ensure the callback runs only once (http://bkaprt.com/rjs39/07-14).

MANAGING THIRD-PARTY JAVASCRIPT **173**

This example could be improved a bit. Like—I don't know—you might not want to load the script when the `div.fb-like` element is *in* view, but rather as it *approaches* the viewport. For this, you can pass the `rootMargin` option to the intersection observer instance (http://bkaprt.com/rjs39/07-15). You could also style the `div.fb-like` element with a `min-height` rule to limit layout shifts as its contents load.

Let it be known that lazy-loading isn't just for images. When it comes to third-party scripts like these that can tax devices during startup, load them lazily whenever practical.

CONTENT SECURITY POLICIES

Sometimes third-party scripts go beyond being mere performance liabilities to something worse. In 2020, the HTTP Archive found that almost 84 percent of mobile pages had at least one vulnerable JavaScript dependency (http://bkaprt.com/rjs39/07-16). In an industry where we tend to install JavaScript packages without much skepticism, that should give you pause.

Thankfully, there's a web platform feature to help protect us from compromised third-party vendors: *Content Security Policy* (CSP). CSP helps with a problem called *cross-site scripting* (XSS), a security vulnerability in which malicious code is injected on a page to gain access to confidential information such as cookie contents, data kept in web storage, or any information accessible through JavaScript APIs.

CSPs are dictated by the `Content-Security-Policy` HTTP header. This header is composed of one or more *policy directives*. These directives describe which origins the current page are allowed to load assets from and which types of assets are allowed, as well as additional rules such as whether inline scripts and styles can be used—the latter of which is pretty damn important in the case of XSS attacks, as those are often done via injected inline `<script>` elements.

While many policy directives could be useful for securing your site against compromised third-party assets, there are too many to list here (http://bkaprt.com/rjs39/07-17). Instead, we'll focus on a handful of the more effective ones.

default-src

Good security policies start with good defaults. For home security, we rely on locks first, then supplement them with additional measures. CSP is no different, and the bedrock of your CSP should be the `default-src` policy directive.

`default-src` is a catch-all that dictates the rules for what can be loaded from where in the absence of other policy directives (which we'll cover soon enough). `default-src` is reasonably strict, with the understanding that this strictness will be supplemented by higher-level policy directives.

A good `default-src` policy may look something like this:

```
Content-Security-Policy: default-src 'self' https:
```

This states that *all* requests should come from the primary origin or any origin serving content over HTTPS. `default-src` also disallows inline `<script>` and `<style>` elements, the former of which can be injected into the DOM to steal sensitive information by an attacker. We'll touch on how you can manage those inline `<script>` elements shortly.

Reminder: `default-src` isn't inherited by other policies, and kicks in only for requests that aren't governed by more specific policies (http://bkaprt.com/rjs39/07-18). If you need specific rules for specific asset types, you'll need to lean on other directives—such as `script-src`.

script-src

`script-src` is what you're after when it comes to mitigating potentially malicious third-party JavaScript. While `default-src` establishes requirements as to where all assets can be loaded from, `script-src` applies only to mechanisms that load script assets and inline script event handlers (e.g., `onload`).

Like other directives, `script-src` takes a space-separated list of keywords or origins that scripts may be loaded from. Multiple policy directives are separated by semicolons. Riffing on our current `default-src`, a `script-src` policy looks like this:

```
Content-Security-Policy: default-src 'self' https:;
  script-src 'self' https://nexus.ensighten.com
```

The `script-src` portion of this CSP says:

- Scripts from the primary origin are allowed.
- Scripts from `nexus.ensighten.com` are allowed.

Enabling CSP also has the intentional (though not obvious) effect of disallowing inline scripts. If a third-party is compromised—or just unscrupulous—their JavaScript could inject a `<script>` element on the page and collect sensitive information from JavaScript APIs for future exploitation.

While `script-src` can be configured to allow inline scripts via the `'unsafe-inline'` flag, that's a bad idea. You can move these scripts into separate files, or you can still use inline scripts if you use a nonce in your CSP header. In cryptography, a *nonce* is a random number to be used only once (http://bkaprt.com/rjs39/07-19).

Regarding CSP, a nonce must be randomly generated on every request as a base64-encoded string (http://bkaprt.com/rjs39/07-20) and sent as part of the `script-src` directive:

```
Content-Security-Policy: script-src 'self' https://
  nexus.ensighten.com 'nonce-aWJ1ZmFiaXVhc2RjYmk='
```

From there, inline `<script>` elements must have their `nonce` attribute set to the same nonce set in the CSP header:

```
<script nonce="aWJ1ZmFiaXVhc2RjYmk=">
  // A trusted inline script
</script>
```

It's not trivial to implement, but then again, security is no trivial matter. Generating nonces requires an application backend. In PHP, this can be done with functions like `random_bytes` (http://bkaprt.com/rjs39/07-21) and `base64_encode` (http://bkaprt.com/rjs39/07-22).

connect-src

As we covered earlier, some third-party scripts may request assets from other cross-origins you don't know about. While it's wise to restrict which cross-origin scripts are loaded via `script-src`, it's also worth restricting which assets *those* scripts load. That's where `connect-src` comes into play.

When it comes to third-party assets, it might not be practical to restrict the `connect-src`'s allowable origins to `'self'`. A decent start may be to restrict resources loaded from scripts from any secure origin. Building on our CSP, here's what that would look like:

```
Content-Security-Policy: default-src 'self' https:;
  script-src 'self' https://nexus.ensighten.com;
  connect-src: 'self' https:
```

This is a start, but consider placing further restrictions on additional cross-origins as you gain better insight into which ones your third-party scripts load other scripts from. This is the most difficult part of crafting a good CSP; it takes time and effort.

Thankfully, there's an approach you can take that doesn't *enforce* a CSP, but merely reports when violations do occur—which is perfect when you want to catch potential CSP violations on a given page, but don't want to inadvertently impact page functionality!

Incremental adoption with CSP reporting

Let's say you're in a situation where you can't enforce a CSP yet, but you'd like to know when violations of it occur. There are two CSP features that can assist you in that effort:

1. The `Content-Security-Policy-Report-Only` header
2. The `report-to` policy directive

The `Content-Security-Policy-Report-Only` header takes the same format as `Content-Security-Policy`, only it doesn't enforce a CSP. Rather, it raises warnings when violations occur. Using this header in conjunction with the `report-to` policy directive lets you transmit violations and their associated data to an endpoint for review.

So, let's say your CSP is working, but you want to refine your `connect-src` policy directive without breaking stuff. Therefore, you've decided to adopt a CSP with a sole `connect-src` policy directive of `'self' https:`, but add the other directives plus a refined `connect-src` policy directive to the `Content-Security-Policy-Report-Only` header:

```
Content-Security-Policy-Report-Only: default-src
  'self' https:; script-src 'self ' https://nexus.
  ensighten.com; connect-src: 'self' https://nexus.
  ensighten.com https://www.googletagmanager.com;
  report-to compuglobalhypermeganet
```

Here, we're saying that scripts are allowed from nexus.ensighten.com and googletagmanager.com, but, knowing how third-party scripts might grab assets from all sorts of cross-origins, we want to be notified if a third-party script requests assets from cross-origins we haven't seen before.

To be notified when violations of this report-only policy do occur, we add an additional `report-to` directive that specifies a group name. A group name can be anything we want so long as it correlates with a JSON payload we send in the accompanying `Report-To` header:

```
Report-To: {"group": "compuglobalhypermeganet",
  "max_age": 3600, "endpoints": [{"url": "https://
  compuglobalhypermega.net/csp-report.php"}]}
```

This JSON payload specifies the following information:

- `group`, which is the group name in the `report-to` directive
- `max_age`, which is how long (in seconds) the browser should send reports to the associated collection endpoint
- `endpoints`, which is an array of endpoints to send collection data to

In this case, the CSP won't be enforced when violations occur, but details of those violations will be reported. From here, we can make an informed decision about how and when the policy can be migrated from `Content-Security-Policy-Report-Only` to `Content-Security-Policy`.

Crafting a CSP is a slow and steady process, but the work pays off in the form of a safer user experience. As performance-focused as this book is, security is also a component of a good user experience, and just one more part of using JavaScript responsibly.

FOREWARNED IS FOREARMED

It's already a slog to make sure our first-party JavaScript isn't goofing things up for users. It can be exhausting to feel like you have to be vigilant not only about threats from within, but also from without.

Yet this is the work we must do. So we need to move with care when it comes to third-party JavaScript we can't control. We must identify JavaScript-borne performance problems, and do our best to remedy them, just as we would for any other hitch in the websites in our charge. More than any other quality, vigilance is truly what it takes to use JavaScript responsibly.

CONCLUSION

WHEN YOU PUT THIS BOOK down and head back to your daily work, I hope you understand that the aim of *Responsible JavaScript* isn't to lament or condemn our industry's collective use of JavaScript but to provide a path for developing more sustainably for the web. We may answer daily to engineering managers, product stakeholders, and our colleagues, but the primary responsibility of our work is to the people we build for.

The web is an indispensable tool that connects people, expedites our daily work, and provides portals to support us during times of crisis. How we choose to use JavaScript affects how people navigate through life.

Ours is a difficult job, one that calls on us to embody the spirit of incremental progress. If your website has issues with JavaScript performance, it's going to take time and effort to get things running smoothly. Do what you can today to make tomorrow a little better for folks, knowing that, over time, you'll make incredible progress.

I wish you—I wish us—luck.

ACKNOWLEDGMENTS

I'VE WRITTEN BOOKS BEFORE, and this book was more work than any of the others. A Book Apart cares about the quality of their materials, and their editorial process reflects that. It's a great honor to be part of such a great publisher's lineup of books and work with the people who make them great.

To kick off this gratitude tour, I'd like to thank Lisa Maria Marquis and Mat Marquis, the power couple behind the editing arm of A Book Apart. Lisa was the best sort of cheerleader. She poked holes in all the places where holes needed to be poked, but also heard out my worst insecurities and fears that come with this kind of project. Mat was a delight to work with. When he wasn't messing with drip pans, keeping bees, dipping into weird botany, or wrangling foodstuffs, he gave this manuscript the proper drubbing it needed.

I solicited a *lot* of help from many talented and knowledgeable people in peer reviewing this manuscript for accuracy and quality. I'd like to extend my sincerest appreciation to Eric Bailey, Zach Leatherman, Brandon Gregory, Yoav Weiss, Houssein Djirdeh, Shubhie Panicker, Olu Niyi-Awosusi, and Eric Portis for their great feedback, which made this book the best possible version of itself that it could be.

I'd also like to thank Paul Calvano, who selflessly offered his time and expertise in querying the HTTP Archive's massive dataset, Tim Kadlec for his work on the 2020 edition of the HTTP Archive's almanac, and Matt Hobbs, whose work on the GOV.UK website offered valuable insight into how browser usage and JavaScript features intersect in such a critical piece of government infrastructure.

Additionally, I'd like to thank Tatiana Mac, Mattia Menchetti, and Kyle Rush for their permission to include references to—and use of—some of their materials in this book.

This book's foreword author, Estelle Weyl, has been a dear friend and colleague whose work and documentation have paved the way for me to write a book of this magnitude. Chances are if you've read something on MDN, she had a hand in it somewhere. I would like to thank her for throwing her kind words of support behind this book, as well as Eric Bailey, Olu Niyi-Awosusi, Katie Sylor-Miller, and Suz Hinton for their kind endorsements of this book.

Finally, I'd like to thank Katel LeDû and Jeffrey Zeldman for the opportunity to write a book under the umbrella of A Book Apart, a publisher whose works have been so groundbreaking, and so influential to me personally. I can't express enough gratitude for this opportunity.

RESOURCES

THIS BOOK COULD NEVER come close to covering everything you need to know about using JavaScript responsibly. You'd need a tome for that, and A Book Apart ain't in the business of tomes. If you find yourself curious about something this book doesn't cover in exacting detail, then this categorized list should come in handy.

Accessibility

- *Accessibility for Everyone* by Laura Kalbag (http://bkaprt.com/rjs39/07-07)
- *The A11Y Project* (http://bkaprt.com/rjs39/08-01)
- *HTML: A Good Basis for Accessibility* by MDN (http://bkaprt.com/rjs39/08-02)
- *Getting Started with ARIA* by Monika Piotrowicz (http://bkaprt.com/rjs39/08-03)
- Web Content Accessibility Guidelines (WCAG) Overview by W3C Web Accessibility Initiative (http://bkaprt.com/rjs39/08-04)

CSS

- *Layout Land* by Jen Simmons (http://bkaprt.com/rjs39/08-05)
- *Get Ready for CSS Grid Layout* by Rachel Andrew (http://bkaprt.com/rjs39/08-06)
- *The New CSS Layout* by Rachel Andrew (http://bkaprt.com/rjs39/08-07)
- *Modern CSS Solutions for Old CSS Problems* (http://bkaprt.com/rjs39/08-08)

Observer APIs

- *Now You See Me: How to Defer, Lazy-Load and Act With IntersectionObserver* by Denys Mishunov (http://bkaprt.com/rjs39/08-09)
- *Getting to Know the MutationObserver API* by Louis Lazaris (http://bkaprt.com/rjs39/08-10)
- *ResizeObserver: It's Like document.onresize for Elements* by Surma and Joe Medley (http://bkaprt.com/rjs39/08-11)
- *Performance Observer: Efficient Access to Performance Data* by Marc Cohen (http://bkaprt.com/rjs39/08-12)

Third-party JavaScript

- *Loading Third-Party JavaScript* by Addy Osmani and Arthur Evans (http://bkaprt.com/rjs39/08-13)
- *Things to Know (and Potential Dangers) with Third-Party Scripts* by Yaphi Berhanu (http://bkaprt.com/rjs39/08-14)
- *Third-Party JavaScript Performance* by Milica Mihajlija (http://bkaprt.com/rjs39/08-15)
- *Third-Party JavaScript* by Ben Vinegar and Anton Kovalyov (http://bkaprt.com/rjs39/08-16).

Runtime performance

I could never cover every API or concept that might improve the runtime performance of your projects. This book can only fit so many words in it, so there's a lot of ground out there for you to cover if you're hungry to know more. If that describes you, here's a few starting points:

- Your framework choices have an impact on the main thread beyond startup. I tested React versus Preact versus native event listener performance across an array of devices (http://bkaprt.com/rjs39/08-17). It bears emphasizing that Preact was several times better than React for runtime performance using the same API. It may seem like a trivial benchmark, but the costs of stateful client-side components scale up very quickly and sometimes disastrously. *Always* weigh framework choices with care.
- If you have experience with C/C++ or Rust, Web Assembly (WASM) is a platform feature that allows you to interface with WASM-targeted binaries in JavaScript. The Squoosh app I mentioned in Chapter 6 uses tons of WASM binaries to optimize images in the browser (http://bkaprt.com/rjs39/08-18).
- If you like to do generative artwork in the browser, you're probably familiar with the `<canvas>` API. A relatively new technology called the CSS Paint API uses a specialized sort of web worker called a paint worklet, which uses the 2D canvas context and lets you draw artwork and embed it in a CSS `background-image` property. Paint worklets can also be customized with CSS (http://bkaprt.com/rjs39/08-19).

REFERENCES

Shortened URLs are numbered sequentially; the related long URLs are listed below for reference.

Chapter 1

- 01-01 https://commons.wikimedia.org/wiki/File:Sphex_pensylvanicus.jpg
- 01-02 https://creativecommons.org/publicdomain/zero/1.0/deed.en
- 01-03 https://www.worldwidewords.org/weirdwords/ww-sph3.htm
- 01-04 https://httparchive.org/reports/state-of-javascript#bytesJs
- 01-05 https://www.w3.org/TR/html-design-principles/#priority-of-constituencies
- 01-06 https://github.com/HTTPArchive/httparchive.org/blob/518b-6de28e11063cb24187917960bef757d1d21f/docs/gettingstarted_bigquery.md
- 01-07 https://www.gsmarena.com/blu_studio_mini-9877.php
- 01-08 https://en.wikipedia.org/wiki/Thread_(computing)
- 01-09 https://developer.mozilla.org/en-US/docs/Web/API/Web_Workers_API/Using_web_workers
- 01-10 https://web.dev/rail/#50-ms-or-100-ms
- 01-11 https://developers.google.com/web/fundamentals/performance/rendering#60fps_and_device_refresh_rates
- 01-12 https://github.com/w3c/longtasks
- 01-13 http://www.timberjay.com/stories/no-easy-options-for-greenwood,17807
- 01-14 https://commons.wikimedia.org/wiki/File:Laptop_Heatsink.jpg
- 01-15 https://creativecommons.org/licenses/by-sa/4.0
- 01-16 https://en.wikipedia.org/wiki/ARM_Cortex-A7
- 01-17 https://www.pewresearch.org/internet/2015/11/19/2-job-seeking-in-the-era-of-smartphones-and-social-media/

Chapter 2

- 02-01 https://developer.mozilla.org/en-US/docs/Web/JavaScript/Reference/Global_Objects/Array/filter
- 02-02 https://developer.mozilla.org/en-US/docs/Web/JavaScript/Reference/Global_Objects/Array/reduce
- 02-03 https://developer.mozilla.org/en-US/docs/Web/JavaScript/Reference/Global_Objects/Array/concat

02-04 https://javascript.info/keys-values-entries
02-05 https://developer.mozilla.org/en-US/docs/Web/JavaScript/Reference/Global_Objects
02-06 https://2020.stateofjs.com/en-US/
02-07 https://timkadlec.com/remembers/2020-04-21-the-cost-of-javascript-frameworks/#javascript-bytes
02-08 https://blog.webpagetest.org/posts/benchmarking-javascript-memory-usage/
02-09 https://github.com/a11yproject/a11yproject.com/blob/fdd74aa7a49faff94bda363ad7528e8cb41ede68/TECHNOLOGY.md
02-10 https://www.selfdefined.app/
02-11 https://developers.google.com/web/updates/2019/02/rendering-on-the-web#server-vs-static
02-12 https://html.spec.whatwg.org/multipage/history.html%23history
02-13 https://www.deque.com/blog/accessibility-tips-in-single-page-applications/
02-14 https://infrequently.org/2018/09/the-developer-experience-bait-and-switch/
02-15 https://developer.mozilla.org/en-US/docs/Web/HTTP/Headers/Cache-Control
02-16 https://alistapart.com/article/understandingprogressiveenhancement/
02-17 https://css-tricks.com/radeventlistener-a-tale-of-client-side-framework-performance/#google-chrome-on-nokia-2
02-18 https://html.spec.whatwg.org/%23attr-is

Chapter 3

03-01 https://commons.wikimedia.org/wiki/File:Horse_guard_wasp.jpg
03-02 https://creativecommons.org/licenses/by/3.0/us/deed.en
03-03 https://webmasters.googleblog.com/2020/05/evaluating-page-experience.html
03-04 https://web.dev/lcp/#what-is-a-good-lcp-score
03-05 https://web.dev/cls/#layout-shift-score
03-06 https://crystallize.com/blog/frontend-performance-react-ssr-and-the-uncanny-valley
03-07 https://web.dev/tti/#what-is-a-good-tti-score
03-08 https://developer.mozilla.org/en-US/docs/Web/API/Long_Tasks_API

03-09 https://github.com/malchata/grab-vitals/blob/fbc7000bd-765c44f40699d97fdd86b53ddf2c805/src/lib/report-metrics.js#L17-L42

03-10 https://web.dev/fid/#what-is-a-good-fid-score

03-11 https://web.dev/tbt/#what-is-a-good-tbt-score

03-12 https://en.wikipedia.org/wiki/Unreachable_code

03-13 https://v8.dev/blog/preparser

03-14 https://blog.teamtreehouse.com/introduction-source-maps

03-15 https://developer.mozilla.org/en-US/docs/Web/API/User_Timing_API

03-16 https://developer.android.com/studio/debug/dev-options#enable

03-17 https://developer.apple.com/library/archive/documentation/NetworkingInternetWeb/Conceptual/Web_Inspector_Tutorial/EnableWebInspector/EnableWebInspector.html

03-18 https://gs.statcounter.com/os-market-share

03-19 https://github.com/akamai/boomerang

03-20 https://www.npmjs.com/package/grab-vitals

03-21 https://developer.mozilla.org/en-US/docs/Web/API/Window/requestIdleCallback

03-22 https://github.com/malchata/grab-vitals/blob/ed7687a8b5b2ac-95cb04a9d9159d89fe7379c905/src/lib/grab-vitals.js#L33-L48

03-23 https://web.dev/disallow-synchronous-xhr/

03-24 https://github.com/malchata/grab-vitals/blob/ed7687a8b5b2ac-95cb04a9d9159d89fe7379c905/README.md%23handling-metrics-in-your-application-back-end

03-25 https://www.igvita.com/2016/01/12/the-average-page-is-a-myth/

Chapter 4

04-01 http://www.mattiamenchetti.com/

04-02 https://v8.dev/features/dynamic-import

04-03 https://web.dev/reduce-javascript-payloads-with-code-splitting/

04-04 https://almanac.httparchive.org/en/2020/javascript%23how-much-javascript-do-we-use

04-05 https://bundlephobia.com/result?p=moment@2.29.1

04-06 https://formatjs.io/docs/polyfills/intl-relativetimeformat/#dynamic-import--capability-detection

04-07 https://caniuse.com/

04-08 https://en.wikipedia.org/wiki/TCP_congestion_control#Slow_start

04-09 https://cdnjs.com/

04-10 https://andydavies.me/blog/2018/09/06/safari-caching-and-3rd-party-resources/
04-11 https://calibreapp.com/blog/critical-request
04-12 https://docs.google.com/document/d/1ZEi-XXhpajrnq8oqs5SiW-CXR-3jMc20jWIzN5QRy1QA/edit?usp=sharing
04-13 https://www.w3.org/TR/preload/#as-attribute
04-14 https://developers.google.com/web/updates/2017/12/modulepreload
04-15 https://maps.psc.wi.gov/apps/WisconsinBroadbandMap/
04-16 https://developer.mozilla.org/en-US/docs/Web/API/Window/localStorage
04-17 https://developer.mozilla.org/en-US/docs/Web/API/Service_Worker_API
04-18 https://developers.google.com/web/updates/2017/02/navigation-preload
04-19 https://alistapart.com/article/now-thats-what-i-call-service-worker/
04-20 https://developer.mozilla.org/en-US/docs/Web/API/Cache
04-21 https://developer.mozilla.org/en-US/docs/Web/API/ServiceWorkerGlobalScope/install_event
04-22 https://developer.mozilla.org/en-US/docs/Web/API/CacheStorage/open
04-23 https://developer.mozilla.org/en-US/docs/Web/API/Cache/addAll
04-24 https://github.com/malchata/service-worker-example/blob/ff26f5e3313d-6afc340afafd6265ecb2ca10a287/rollup.config.js#L14-L17
04-25 https://developer.mozilla.org/en-US/docs/Web/API/CacheStorage/keys
04-26 https://developer.mozilla.org/en-US/docs/Web/API/CacheStorage/delete
04-27 https://developer.mozilla.org/en-US/docs/Web/API/Cache/match
04-28 https://github.com/malchata/service-worker-example/blob/4c900a30e40b275e086d507034658987f399beb0/lib/merge-responses.js
04-29 https://developer.mozilla.org/en-US/docs/Web/API/ReadableStream
04-30 https://caniuse.com/serviceworkers

Chapter 5

05-01 https://commons.wikimedia.org/wiki/File:Eastern_Cicada_Killer_(Sphecius_speciosus)_with_Cicada_-_Bles_Park,_Va.jpg
05-02 https://creativecommons.org/licenses/by/2.0/deed.en
05-03 https://gulpjs.com/
05-04 https://github.com/a11yproject/a11yproject.com/blob/fdd74aa7a49faff94b-da363ad7528e8cb41ede68/TECHNOLOGY.md#prefer
05-05 https://webpack.js.org/
05-06 https://rollupjs.org/
05-07 https://parceljs.org/

05-08 https://web.dev/commonjs-larger-bundles/
05-09 https://babeljs.io/docs/en/babel-preset-env
05-10 https://gomakethings.com/articles/
05-11 https://webpack.js.org/configuration/externals/
05-12 https://babeljs.io/docs/en/assumptions
05-13 https://tc39.es/process-document/
05-14 https://babeljs.io/blog/2018/07/27/removing-babels-stage-presets
05-15 https://caniuse.com/es6-class
05-16 https://github.com/browserslist/browserslist
05-17 https://babeljs.io/docs/en/babel-preset-env#targets
05-18 https://github.com/browserslist/browserslist#query-composition
05-19 https://caniuse.com/es6
05-20 https://www.npmjs.com/package/browserslist-ga
05-21 https://docs.google.com/spreadsheets/d/12l-XO_5IEHxdOvBdR4gEPq1y-Q8JJIdJ4Cpmr9tJKEmc/edit?usp=sharing
05-22 https://babeljs.io/docs/en/babel-preset-env#targetsesmodules
05-23 https://calendar.perfplanet.com/2018/doing-differential-serving-in-2019/
05-24 https://vimeo.com/331573291
05-25 https://github.com/malchata/differential-serving
05-26 https://gist.github.com/jakub-g/5fc11af85a061ca29cc84892f1059fec
05-27 https://jeremy.codes/blog/a-less-risky-differential-serving-pattern/
05-28 https://www.npmjs.com/package/browserslist-useragent
05-29 https://dev.to/thejohnstew/differential-serving-3dkf#alternative-approach
05-30 https://www.igvita.com/2014/05/20/script-injected-async-scripts-considered-harmful/

Chapter 6

06-01 https://commons.wikimedia.org/wiki/File:Vespa_crabo_HC2.jpg
06-02 https://creativecommons.org/licenses/by-sa/3.0
06-03 https://codepen.io/malchata/pen/RwGYYaE
06-04 https://css-tricks.com/introduction-fr-css-unit/
06-05 https://caniuse.com/css-grid
06-06 https://labs.jensimmons.com/
06-07 https://github.com/malchata/yall.js/tree/b6a261117db12957ce-90c9538532538873e3644b#what-about-users-without-javascript
06-08 https://github.com/malchata/yall.js/blob/09e5a2e5adfac1a35bb-28741593d0e6e993a514d/src/yall.mjs#L19
06-09 https://caniuse.com/loading-lazy-attr

06-10 https://www.smashingmagazine.com/2019/05/hybrid-lazy-loading-progressive-migration-native/
06-11 https://developer.mozilla.org/en-US/docs/Web/API/IntersectionObserver/IntersectionObserver#parameters
06-12 https://philipwalton.com/articles/idle-until-urgent/
06-13 https://www.npmjs.com/package/idlize
06-14 https://caniuse.com/requestidlecallback
06-15 https://developer.mozilla.org/en-US/docs/Web/API/Background_Tasks_API
06-16 https://github.com/Financial-Times/polyfill-library/blob/master/polyfills/requestIdleCallback/polyfill.js
06-17 https://developer.mozilla.org/en-US/docs/Web/JavaScript/Reference/Global_Objects/ArrayBuffer
06-18 https://github.com/mattiasw/ExifReader
06-19 https://github.com/malchata/web-worker-example
06-20 https://github.com/malchata/web-worker-example/tree/without-worker
06-21 https://github.com/malchata/web-worker-example/tree/with-worker
06-22 https://developer.mozilla.org/en-US/docs/Web/API/WorkerGlobalScope/importScripts
06-23 https://web.dev/module-workers/#enter-module-workers
06-24 https://developer.mozilla.org/en-US/docs/Web/API/Worker/postMessage
06-25 https://www.npmjs.com/package/comlink
06-26 https://surma.dev/
06-27 https://github.com/mapbox/mapbox-gl-js
06-28 https://squoosh.app/
06-29 https://github.com/ampproject/worker-dom

Chapter 7

07-01 https://commons.wikimedia.org/wiki/File:Yellow_Paper_Wasp.jpg
07-02 http://creativecommons.org/licenses/by-sa/3.0/
07-03 https://developer.mozilla.org/en-US/docs/Web/API/Navigator/deviceMemory
07-04 https://developer.mozilla.org/en-US/docs/Web/API/NavigatorConcurrentHardware/hardwareConcurrency
07-05 https://www.courtlistener.com/docket/4615111/1/guillermo-robles-v-dominos-pizza-llc/
07-06 https://www.tpgi.com/bolt-on-accessibility-5-gears-in-reverse/

07-07   https://abookapart.com/products/accessibility-for-everyone
07-08   https://abookapart.com/products/just-enough-research
07-09   https://medium.com/caspertechteam/we-shaved-1-7-seconds-off-casper-com-by-self-hosting-optimizely-2704bcbff8ec
07-10   https://en.wikipedia.org/wiki/Flash_of_unstyled_content
07-11   https://twitter.com/kylerush
07-12   https://requestmap.webperf.tools/
07-13   https://developer.mozilla.org/en-US/docs/Web/API/Document/createElement
07-14   https://developer.mozilla.org/en-US/docs/Web/API/IntersectionObserver/disconnect
07-15   https://developer.mozilla.org/en-US/docs/Web/API/Intersection_Observer_API#Intersection_observer_options
07-16   https://almanac.httparchive.org/en/2020/javascript#security-vulnerabilities
07-17   https://developer.mozilla.org/en-US/docs/Web/HTTP/Headers/Content-Security-Policy#Directives
07-18   https://developer.mozilla.org/en-US/docs/Web/HTTP/Headers/Content-Security-Policy/default-src#examples
07-19   https://en.wikipedia.org/wiki/Cryptographic_nonce
07-20   https://en.wikipedia.org/wiki/Base64
07-21   https://www.php.net/random_bytes
07-22   https://www.php.net/base64_encode

Resources

08-01   https://www.a11yproject.com/
08-02   https://developer.mozilla.org/en-US/docs/Learn/Accessibility/HTML
08-03   https://www.a11yproject.com/posts/2014-05-15-getting-started-aria/
08-04   https://www.w3.org/WAI/standards-guidelines/wcag/
08-05   https://www.youtube.com/layoutland
08-06   https://abookapart.com/products/get-ready-for-css-grid-layout
08-07   https://abookapart.com/products/the-new-css-layout
08-08   https://moderncss.dev/
08-09   https://www.smashingmagazine.com/2018/01/deferring-lazy-loading-intersection-observer-api/

08-10 https://www.smashingmagazine.com/2019/04/mutationobserver-api-guide/
08-11 https://web.dev/resize-observer/
08-12 https://developers.google.com/web/updates/2016/06/performance-observer
08-13 https://developers.google.com/web/fundamentals/performance/optimizing-content-efficiency/loading-third-party-javascript
08-14 https://css-tricks.com/potential-dangers-of-third-party-javascript/
08-15 https://web.dev/third-party-javascript/
08-16 https://www.manning.com/books/third-party-javascript
08-17 https://css-tricks.com/radeventlistener-a-tale-of-client-side-framework-performance/
08-18 https://github.com/GoogleChromeLabs/squoosh
08-19 https://paintlets.herokuapp.com/

INDEX

A

A11Y Project 22, 145
accessibility overlays 164
app shell 27
architecture documentation 21-22
asset manifest 99

B

bandwagon fallacy 18-21
browserslist 124-127
bundlers 111-117
bundling and delivery 127-132

C

Casselmann, Holger 135
client-side A/B testing frameworks 162
client-side routing and accessibility 30-31
code splitting 76-78
CommonJS modules 113
content delivery network (CDN) 32
content security policies 174-178
critical path 84
cross-site scripting (XSS) 174
CSS and HTML 135-140

D

data saving 90-96
deferred behavior 77
dependency graph 112
dynamic imports 76

E

entry points 112
ES modules (ESM) 113
establishing early connections 168-170
Evans, Howard Ensign 47
externalizing dependencies 116-117

F

feature delivery 74-80
Ferdinandi, Chris 116
First Input Delay (FID) 53
first-party JavaScript 160
flame chart 57
frame 10

G

Gallagher, Judy 110

H

Hall, Erika 167
Hearne, Simon 169-170
heatmaps 165-167
Hofstadter, Douglas 1
HTTP/3 81

I

idle callbacks 144-147
idle time 144-150

K

Kadlec, Tim 19
Kalbag, Laura 165

L

layout stability 50-51
    Cumulative Layout Shift (CLS) 51
lazy loading 138-140
lazy parsing 62
loading performance 59-62
long task 10

M

main-thread responsiveness metrics
    52-55
measuring JavaScript performance
    47-54
Menchetti, Mattia 73
metrics
    field 48, 68-72
    lab 48

O

observer APIs 140-143

P

painting 48-50
    First Contentful Paint (FCP) 49
    First Paint (FP) 49
    Largest Contentful Paint (LCP) 49
performance 4-6
    device 11-13
    loading 4
    runtime 5
performance profiler
    populated 56-58
performance profilers 55-67
platforms over libraries 17-18
policy directives 174
polyfilling features 78-80
progressive enhancement 35-44

R

ransmission control protocol (TCP) 81
request chains 169
resource hints 83-90
runtime performance 63-64

S

self-hosting 81-82, 167-168
sensible caching 31-34
server-first approach 26-29
Service Workers 96-108
shared caching 82
Simmons, Jen 138
Single-Page Application (SPA) 30
Sphex 1
static assets 33
static imports 75
Sutton, Marcy 31

T

task runners 110-111
TC39 committee 122
technology statement 21
testing on devices 65-68
thermal throttling 11
third-party JavaScript 160
threads 7-10
Time to Interactive (TTI) 52
Total Blocking Time (TBT) 54
transforms 118-122
transpiler 114
transpilers 117-127
transport layer security (TLS) 81
tree shaking 112-116

W

Walton, Phil 149
Web Components 38
websites vs. web apps 23-25
web workers 151-156
worker thread 151

ABOUT A BOOK APART

We cover the emerging and essential topics in web design and development with style, clarity, and above all, brevity—because working designer-developers can't afford to waste time.

COLOPHON

The text is set in FF Yoga and its companion, FF Yoga Sans, both by Xavier Dupré. Headlines and cover are set in Titling Gothic by David Berlow.

This book was printed in the United States using FSC certified papers.